IPM for Gardeners

IPM for Gardeners

A Guide to Integrated Pest Management

Raymond A. Cloyd,
Philip L. Nixon,
and Nancy R. Pataky

Timber Press
Portland • Cambridge

Published in 2004 by
Timber Press, Inc.
The Haseltine Building
133 S.W. Second Avenue, Suite 450
Portland, Oregon 97204-3527, U.S.A.

Timber Press
2 Station Road
Swavesey
Cambridge CB4 5QJ, U.K.

www.timberpress.com

Printed in China

Library of Congress Cataloging-in-Publication Data

Cloyd, Raymond A.
        IPM for gardeners : a guide to integrated pest management /
    Raymond A. Cloyd, Philip L. Nixon, and Nancy R. Pataky.
            p.   cm.
    Includes bibliographical references (p.   ).
    ISBN 0-88192-647-7 (hardback)
        1. Garden pests—Integrated control. I. Nixon, Philip L. II. Pataky, Nancy R.
    III. Title.
    SB603.5.C58   2004
    632.9—dc22
                                                                                2003023791

A catalog record for this book is also available from the British Library.

Contents

Color plates follow page 32

What Is IPM?

Integrated pest management, or IPM, came about primarily as a result of Rachel Carson's seminal book, *Silent Spring*. First published in 1962, Carson's book addressed a number of issues related to pesticide use in both agricultural settings and home landscapes. Prior to its publication, the application of pesticides was often the only method used to manage insects, mites, and diseases; however, continued reliance on pesticides gave rise to resistant pest populations and undesirable environmental effects. In *Silent Spring*, Carson exposed how pesticides were being used indiscriminately without any thought to their environmental impact, and this realization led to philosophical changes in the management of insects, mites, and diseases in landscapes and gardens.

Although Carson dealt primarily with the negative impacts of pesticides, she never suggested that pesticides be eliminated completely. Rather, she stressed their use only as a last resort when all other pest management options have been exhausted. This led to attempts at other pest management strategies—including use of ornamental plants that are less susceptible to insects, mites, and diseases—with the goal of preserving the natural enemies or beneficial organisms that would normally be killed by pesticide applications.

IPM also focuses on the needs of plants in landscapes and gardens, whether in sun or shade as in plates 1 and 2, so they are better able to defend themselves against insects, mites, and diseases. For example, healthy plants are generally able to produce compounds that prevent extensive insect and mite feeding, or they smother insects once inside tissues. However, when plants in landscapes are stressed as a result of improper cultural practices such as watering, fertilization, mulching, and pruning (as shown in figures 1 through 3), the plant's defense system is compromised. This opens the plant up to attack by opportunistic insects, primarily wood-boring beetles or caterpillars, and disease organisms.

IPM is an approach to dealing with pests—including insects, mites, and diseases—using a single cultural, physical (mechanical), chemical, or biological management strategy, or a combination of strategies. Foremost, it determines the need for action by monitoring pest problems, an approach that leads to an environmentally sound pest management program for landscapes and gardens. In home landscapes, the degree of pest management action taken depends on the amount of aesthetic damage that has been done. Although aesthetic damage can reduce the quality of the landscape, the appearance of a landscape does not necessarily reflect the effectiveness of the pest manage-

Figure 1. Drought- or water-stressed tree. Photo courtesy of Raymond A. Cloyd

Figure 2. Improperly applied mulch, covering crown of plant. Photo courtesy of Raymond A. Cloyd

Figure 3. Pruning stub as a result of an improper pruning cut. Photo courtesy of Raymond A. Cloyd

ment program. With IPM, the combination of environmental and economical management strategies is not aimed at eliminating pests, but rather at keeping pest numbers low enough to minimize plant damage in landscapes and gardens. IPM does not mean the elimination of pesticides; rather, it promotes their use only when needed, that is, after other management options have been exhausted.

IPM strives simply to minimize problems with insects, mites, and diseases by assessing the needs of plants, disease organisms, insects, and mites in landscapes. As a result of this assessment, homeowners gain better understanding of how various IPM strategies function in reducing pest problems. This enables homeowners to implement the appropriate strategy or strategies.

How this book is organized

This book provides a broad view of IPM. Chapters 1 through 3 discuss the needs of plants, diseases, and insect and other pests. The background information in these chapters is critical to understanding why certain IPM strategies are effective. Chapters 4 through 9 outline the four major management strategies that define IPM—cultural, physical, mechanical, and biological—and discusses when these strategies may be appropriate for preventing or man-

Chapter 1

Plant Needs

As we all know, to maintain healthy landscape plants, it is important to manage pests. Equally true, however, is that effective pest management requires a healthy, vigorous plant. These two points cannot be separated, and both are intimately involved in landscape IPM. Before we can even attempt to manage plant pests, it is essential that we understand something about the needs of the host plant.

It is also important to consider the ultimate goal of pest management in a home landscape. Unlike an agricultural setting, where maximum growth rate and yield are the focus, landscapes are intended to be both useful (provide shade, function, added value) and aesthetically pleasing. The goal is not to obtain bigger and better plants as much as to maintain healthy, vigorous plants that are easy to manage, or what is often called *plant health care*. Healthy plants are

- more resistant to attack by insects and diseases
- more likely to recover from environmental and other stresses
- better able to withstand injury

Therefore, it is best to rely on healthy plant growth and development as one deterrent to plant problems. Not surprisingly, IPM is closely tied to plant health.

Understanding plant growth and development

To discuss plant needs, we need a working understanding of plant growth, differentiation, and development. *Plant growth* is the irreversible increase in either the mass or size of cells. By definition, true growth occurs only in living organisms. Because growth is quantitative, it is easy to measure. In vegetable production, for example, increases in dry or fresh weight are frequently used to measure growth.

Differentiation refers to differences other than size that occur in the process of cell, tissue, or organ changes as cells multiply. One cell divides to form

---

Measuring tree growth

Arborists often use the increase in new stem length as a measure of growth in a tree. Because the newest growth is often lighter in color, it is easy to distinguish from older growth. The amount of growth from the stem tip to the place on the stem where a series of closely spaced lines encircles the stem (last year's *bud scale scar*) reflects one year's growth. The scar is left where the bud scales on the bud at the branch tip were connected. This terminal bud is usually the largest and therefore leaves a prominent scar on the stem. The distance from that bud scale scar to the next bud scale scar reflects the previous year's growth, as shown in plate 3.

It is possible to assess tree growth over the past few years by looking at the amount of stem growth between bud scale scars, and this is a common diagnostic tool when assessing tree health. Several years of stressful conditions may produce only 1 inch of new stem growth, whereas a single year of healthy development may result in 10 to12 inches of stem growth for that year alone. Tree identification references often list the amount of annual growth that one can expect depending on species. Because soil and environmental conditions will influence growth, be sure to use a reference intended for your region.

It is possible to measure growth in other ways as well. For example, a cross section of a tree trunk exposes growth rings in the wood (secondary xylem, the water-conducting tissues). The width of these rings provides a comparative measurement of growth, and stressful years are easy to differentiate.

two cells that may develop into different tissues. For example, general plant cells may give rise to water-conducting vessels, or phloem sieve tubes that move organic matter in the plant, or even epidermal cells. Differentiation is qualitative: Although one can see changes as new tissues emerge and the plant takes form, the changes are difficult to measure.

Development takes into account both growth and differentiation. It represents the sum of all changes that a plant undergoes in life. Because these changes are closely interrelated, "plant growth and development" is generally accepted terminology, even though it is somewhat redundant.

Plant development is not always productive. Plants do not increase in size, shape, and volume without limits. Although plants such as kudzu (*Pueraria lobata*), tree-of-heaven (*Ailanthus altissima*), and other weedy ornamentals certainly have a high degree of productive metabolism, these plants do not experience unlimited growth. Even plants that appear to be thriving have nonproductive growth processes at work as well.

Plant growth and development is described in terms of metabolism. *Metabolism* is the sum of the processes of building up and tearing down the living substance of which cells are composed (the protoplasm). Plant development involves a continual process of metabolism—both anabolic (constructive) and catabolic (destructive). Photosynthesis is anabolic metabolism, but for it to take place, complex molecules must be broken down into simpler parts. If plant energy sources are used, then some catabolic metabolism must occur to attain the necessary components. Stated another way, carbohydrates produced and stored earlier are converted to energy as needed in current processes, but for this anabolic metabolism to occur, tissue must be broken down. Thus catabolic metabolism is a necessary part of growth and development.

When plants are young, there is much more anabolic metabolism than catabolic metabolism, so growth is rapid. When anabolic and catabolic metabolism are equal, growth still occurs, but without a change in size. In this case, growth is mostly involved in tissue repair and maintenance, as one can see on a mature tree when callous tissue forms over a wound or canker. Bonsai trees, such as the one shown in figure 4, are grown in trays or small containers with restricted root systems. The roots and stems are pruned to maintain a mature tree that is less than 3 feet tall.

Watering and fertilizing are important in keeping anabolic metabolism slightly greater than catabolic metabolism. When catabolic metabolism exceeds anabolic metabolism, decline and death take place. The dying process

Figure 4. Bonsai juniper with restricted root system and appropriately pruned stems. Photo courtesy of Philip L. Nixon

in plants may be rapid, as with annual plants, or slow, as with the natural decline of a tree.

Plant growth and development requires the absorption of materials from outside the plant used in combination with materials within the plant. Plants convert these materials to food that they can store or use immediately. Photosynthesis, respiration, and transpiration are the three major functions involved in this process.

Major plant functions in growth and development

PHOTOSYNTHESIS. The building process in the plant, *photosynthesis*, is an example of anabolic metabolism that means literally "to put together with light." Plants, unlike humans, can produce much of their own food internally. They do so during photosynthesis, by taking carbon dioxide, water, and sunlight and converting them to carbohydrates (sugar and starch) and oxygen. Plants use carbohydrates for energy to do other processes, use them as components to make other compounds, or store them for future use. Photosynthesis requires light and in a natural setting occurs during the daylight hours. It is restricted to cells containing chloroplasts and occurs in the mesophyll layer of leaves.

Anything that limits carbon dioxide, water, or light availability will affect photosynthesis and ultimately affect plant health. Probably the most common visible effect is low light. Foliage plants produced in a greenhouse with high light intensity (as well as daily water and fertility needs provided) thrive with large, dark green leaves. When these plants are moved to a home with poor lighting, within a few weeks the new leaves are much smaller and lighter in color. The low light intensity limits photosynthesis, and the plants become very susceptible to overwatering and root rot, as shown in plate 4. In this situation, it is advisable to reduce watering to meet the plant's decreased demand as it adjusts to the new light level. Thus, understanding what is happening to the plant system makes it easier to determine how to manage the external factors.

Respiration. An example of catabolic metabolism, *respiration* is a breaking down process during which some of the stored carbohydrates produced in photosynthesis are converted to energy. This process can occur under both day and night conditions. Although this is a breaking down process, it is necessary to create the components needed for photosynthesis. Respiration occurs in all living plant cells, and it is the opposite of photosynthesis: Carbohydrates (sugar and starch) plus oxygen are converted to carbon dioxide, water, and energy for plant growth.

Many factors, both internal and external, can limit respiration. Young plant material respires more rapidly than older plant material because more of the young plant is physiologically active and has a higher energy need. Older plants or dormant tissues have less need for energy because they respire at a slower rate. They are also more susceptible to insect and disease problems, weather stress, and site limitations.

Transpiration. The loss of water vapor by a plant is called *transpiration*. It involves the movement of water throughout the plant, starting with absorption through the roots, then movement through the plant, and eventually out of the plant via foliage and stems. This movement is responsible for

- transporting minerals from the soil throughout the plant
- cooling the plant through evaporation of water
- moving sugars and plant chemicals within the plant
- maintaining turgor pressure (distension) of the cells (important because growth occurs only in turgid cells)

The two types of transpiration are cuticular and stomatal. The greatest water loss occurs through stomatal transpiration, and only a small amount of water is lost directly through the cuticle.

The plant epidermis is the outermost layer of cells of leaves, flowers, fruit, seed, and young stems and roots. Usually present in its outer walls is a fatty substance (cutin), which creates a protective layer covering stems, leaves, and mature portions of roots. This protective layer is called the cuticle. Although cuticle thickness varies with the host and the environment, the cuticle usually helps the plant to retain moisture and protects the epidermis from desiccation (drying up).

The continuous network of cells that make up the epidermis have tiny openings called stomata. Each opening, or *stoma*, has a guard cell on either side, and these guard cells regulate the movement of water leaving the stoma. When the guard cells are turgid (distended), the stoma opens. After a period of rainfall, the cells become turgid and the stomata open to allow greater loss of water vapor. During periods of drought, the guard cells are not turgid; therefore, the stomata stay closed, and little transpiration occurs.

Factors such as temperature, light, and carbon dioxide also can influence the opening and closing of stomata. Vegetable plants or new growth on bedding plants may wilt on a hot, windy day, but they are usually able to recover in the evening. When the amount of transpiration is greater than the ability of roots to absorb water, then wilting begins. The stomata close and eventually turgor returns, usually when the temperature drops or the sunlight loses intensity. If a root disease, vascular disease, or boring insect is present, then water may be further limited and the plants may not recover.

Protective benefits of the cuticle

In addition to protecting the epidermis and helping the plant to retain moisture, the cuticle helps to prevent insect and fungal penetration. Tender, new leaves are more susceptible to infection by fungi and invasion by insects because the cuticle is not yet thickened. Anthracnose diseases of trees commonly occur in early spring when weather conditions are ideal for the fungus and the host leaves are most susceptible.

Factors that affect plant growth and development

Knowing about the basic needs of plants naturally leads to an understanding of the minimal requirements for plant survival. In the home landscape setting, however, we are interested in more than plant survival: We desire plants that are aesthetically pleasing and easy to maintain. Homeowners typically consider trees to be permanent and would prefer not to do any regular maintenance. In addition, homeowners may prefer to avoid the use of pesticides. Plants in the landscape need to be healthy to help ward off future pest problems. Therefore, in addition to understanding basic plant needs, it is equally important to understand the factors that affect plant needs. A major focus of IPM in the landscape is plant health, which minimizes many plant problems.

Internal influences over plant growth

Plant growth and development is affected by both internal and external factors. Internal factors include the plant's genetic makeup, nutritional and hormonal balance, connectivity between plant parts, and periodic nature of growth. Thus, internal factors are conditions within the host plant and are difficult to control. In fact, some internal factors are beyond human control. For example, the internal factors affecting growth cannot be altered. Still, it helps to understand these factors when looking at plant health and ways to encourage plant growth.

Genetic makeup

A plant's genetic makeup determines most of its structural or physical attributes, such as color of foliage, pattern of branching, and fall color. Little can be done, short of plant breeding, to change these attributes. Landscapers rely on this fact when they select specific plants to meet site restrictions or design constraints, such as:

- choosing a specific cultivar of crabapple for its flower color
- using a *fastigiate* form of tree (tree with branches that are erect and close together) in an area with limited space for the tree canopy, as shown in figure 5

Figure 5. Trees with fastigiate form are used to fit the available planting site. Photo courtesy of James C. Schmidt

- planting dwarf varieties of evergreens near entryways, as shown in figure 6, to maintain a low planting without the expense of keeping plants pruned to a certain height

Occasionally the environment can manipulate a genetic factor, such as the flower color for some plant species. For example, hydrangeas prefer an acidic soil but will grow in some of the more alkaline soils in the Midwest. With some *Hydrangea* species, the flower color depends on the soil acidity and the amount of aluminum available to the plant. Plants grown in low pH (acidic) soils where aluminum is more available will have blue flowers. The same plants grown in a neutral or alkaline soil with less available aluminum will have pink flowers. The genetic makeup of the hydrangea is what provides it with the ability to exhibit different flower colors. It is therefore important to consider what is known about the genetic makeup of plants, both when selecting plants and when managing landscape problems.

Nutritional balance

Although it has a direct effect on plant growth, the internal nutritional balance for each plant species is predetermined and cannot be altered. We can best directly help the plant with its nutritional needs by providing a balanced supply of inorganic salts (nutrients). Sometimes it is also necessary to alter the soil pH or other factors that are interfering with the plant's ability to absorb nutrients; therefore, it helps to know the needs or peculiarities of the specific

Figure 6. Dwarf evergreens used near a building entryway maintain a low-profile planting with reduced labor expenses. Photo courtesy of Nancy R. Pataky

plant species. Some plants, such as the garden tomato, will grow healthy foliage but will not fruit when supplied with excessive nitrogen levels. Tomato fruit production will resume when nitrogen levels are reduced.

The growth of pin oaks (*Quercus palustris*) is influenced by low iron availability under high soil pH conditions. Under these conditions, the leaves of these trees become very chlorotic (yellowed), as shown in plate 5, and the trees become weak and susceptible to cankers, dieback, and decline. Once the tree receives iron in sufficient quantities, or once the soil pH is lowered, the tree will resume production of dark green leaves and may recover if damage has been minimal.

Plant hormones

Phytohormones are growth substances that occur naturally in the plant and may influence many developmental events. The five groups of plant hormones are auxins, gibberellins, cytokinins, abscisic acid, and ethylene. These hormones affect a range of growth aspects, including

- root and stem growth
- leaf abscission (shedding of leaves)
- flower and fruit production
- dominance of particular plant parts in plant growth
- seed germination
- production of abnormal growths such as galls

One of the more common examples of a phytohormone is auxin. Auxin is present in the terminal bud and is a major factor in suppressing growth of axillary buds (side buds)—what is known as apical dominance. When the terminal bud is removed, axillary buds will develop, producing a bushier, multi-branched plant. The common horticultural practice of pinching capitalizes on this phenomenon to create bushier garden chrysanthemums, and a variety of other landscape garden plants can benefit from it also.

Growth hormones are now produced commercially for use in many ways in the horticulture industry. For example, in table grape production, growers spray a gibberellin formulation onto the grape plants in the early stages of flowering to reduce flower numbers and thereby enlarge fruit size. Also, the application of synthetic auxins promotes roots in the commercial production of plant cuttings. Phytohormones are also useful as herbicides and as sprays to prevent fruit production. For example, the fruit of the ginkgo tree (*Ginkgo biloba*) can be foul smelling and messy after it drops to the ground. Phytohormone-containing products may be sprayed on these trees in urban areas to prevent fruit production and thereby avoid this nuisance.

Other internal factors

Two other internal influences on plant growth are not clearly understood: the internal connections between various plant parts, and the periodic nature of plant growth. The internal connections between various plant parts cannot always be explained physiologically. Phytohormones and competition for nutrients and water only partially explain the connectivity between various plant parts. For example, in most annual plants, flower and fruit formation signals the end of vegetative growth. In some plants, tendrils develop into leaves if normal leaf production is cut short due to injury.

Also not completely understood is the periodicity of growth. The rate at which a cell, an organ, or a plant grows is not uniform; rather, growth starts out slowly, increases to a maximum, and then tapers off. Temperature and other external factors may cause some irregularities in growth, but the growth rate *pattern* will not vary. Perennial plants, for example, follow the same periodicity of growth during each season of growth.

External influences over plant growth

Plant growth and development is also affected by the availability of air, radiation (light), water, temperature, and inorganic salts (nutrients). Because plant growth and development is a continuous process of photosynthesis, respiration, and transpiration, the external factors, or stresses, that affect these processes directly impact plant growth and development.

Air

Carbon dioxide is needed for photosynthesis, oxygen is needed for respiration, and there is an ample supply of each in the atmosphere. Because the stomata provide the major routes for oxygen and carbon dioxide to enter and leave the plant, any factor that influences the opening and closing of stomata can inhibit the movement of these gases and thus limit their supply. Water vapor is also lost through the stomata. The stomata must allow entry of carbon dioxide into the leaf while preventing excessive water loss and desiccation. More than 90 percent of the water vapor and carbon dioxide exchange between a plant and the atmosphere occurs via the stomata.

Extensive study of the complexities of stomatal operation has shown that a complex interaction of light, carbon dioxide levels, plant water status, and temperature influences the operation of stomata. Sometimes these factors conflict. For example, during a period of drought, the stomata will be closed to retain needed moisture. And although high light intensities and buildup of interior oxygen usually cause stomata to open, these influences will not cause stomata to open during drought. Instead, the plant will either retard or shut down the photosynthesis process.

Light

Visible light in particular may be the most important factor in plant growth. Plants need to produce their own food through photosynthesis, and light is the necessary energy component of that process. Light is a constant factor in plant growth from germination to maturity. In fact, organisms other than green plants also ultimately depend on light because they must eventually depend on compounds synthesized by green plants. Thus the energy for life is derived from sunlight. Three factors of light to consider for their effect on

The solar spectrum

Sunlight is the major source of light energy that plants use. The solar spectrum is composed of a range of wavelengths grouped as visible light and invisible radiation in the form of infrared and ultraviolet radiation. Plants primarily use the visible light spectrum. The wavelength of light determines its color, and visible light is radiation of approximately 400 to 700 nanometers. Light also has an energy level depending on wavelength, and the visible light region of the spectrum contains the greatest energy.

plant growth are intensity, quality, and duration, and these factors vary with the season, the time of day, and the weather.

LIGHT INTENSITY. Plants differ in their relative needs for sunlight or shade, but the reason for these differences is not simply a matter of the light required for photosynthesis. For example, plants in a shady location require less nitrogen, and plants with a higher nitrogen requirement may not thrive in shaded sites. The rate of photosynthesis, type of rooting, and acidity of cell sap are a few factors that have been implicated in species adaptation to sun or shade.

However, it is clear that some plants grow best in sun, some grow best in shade, and some thrive in sun but will survive in shade. In the landscape and garden, species known to thrive in sun include yarrow (*Achillea*), *Zinnia*, cock's-comb (*Celosia*), and marigold (*Tagetes*); those that thrive in shade include *Hosta* (plate 6), Japanese pachysandra (*Pachysandra terminalis*), bleeding heart (*Dicentra*), lungwort (*Pulmonaria*), and violet (*Viola*). To avoid problems associated with light stress, try to select plants suited to the planting site.

Numerous plant symptoms may be indicative of improper light intensity; however, these symptoms may result from other stresses as well. Low light intensity often causes stem elongation with thin and undifferentiated leaves, as well as poorly developed roots. High light intensity results in thicker stems with better tissue differentiation, but too much light often causes plants to appear short and stocky with small leaves that are much more compact and thicker than normal.

Light stress with plantings around a new home

It is particularly important to consider light stress when establishing a planting around a new home because often there are few trees to offer shade. Consequently, it would seem logical to select plants that thrive in full sun. As trees mature, however, the shade level increases and smaller plants may begin to decline due to lack of light. One option is to prune nearby plants to provide more light to understory plants. Another is to replace understory plants with those that are shade tolerant. It also may be possible to find plants that will grow in sun or shade.

A good example is when flower or vegetable seedlings are grown indoors for early spring transplanting into the garden. Because of low light conditions indoors, artificial lights need to be as close to the seedlings as possible without touching them. If the light source is too far away, then seedlings will be stretched with weak stems, unable to survive transplanting to the outdoors. If lights are kept close to the seedlings but moved up as the plants grow, then seedlings will have a thick stem and normal sized leaves.

LIGHT QUALITY. The composition of the light spectrum is called *light quality*. Even the quality of sunlight can vary depending on the quality of the atmosphere, the presence or absence of cloud cover, and the time of the day. Unless both fluorescent and incandescent lights are used, plants grown under artificial lights indoors will produce a different type of growth than plants grown in natural light. Fluorescent light has high blue-light content and low red-light content. Incandescent light is high in the red- and infrared-light range but low in the blue-light range. Incandescent lights also generate much more heat, which is not always desirable. Often, growers use both sources of light for plants grown indoors, to duplicate the quality of growth of plants grown in natural light.

LIGHT DURATION. *Photoperiodism* describes how plants grow in response to the duration of light, which affects the

- flowering of tubers and bulbs
- growth habits of annuals, biennials, and perennials
- flowering dates
- character and extent of branching, root growth, abscission, and leaf fall
- dormancy and regrowth

Day length is regulated by the angle of Earth's axis in relation to the Sun. The longest day is June 21, and thereafter day length slowly decreases until December 21, when it begins to increase slowly again. The number of daylight hours can influence flower formation. *Long-day plants* bloom in midsummer when days are long. *Short-day plants* bloom in fall or early spring. The length of the uninterrupted dark period is critical in determining flower initiation. Examples of short-day plants include *Kalanchoe*, *Chrysanthemum*, and poinsettia (*Euphorbia pulcherrima*).

Long-day plants bloom when days are long (or nights are short). Examples include lettuce, spinach, and radish. Some plants, such as tomato, flower not in response to day lengths but instead in response to other stimuli. These are called day-neutral plants. *Phytochrome* is a blue-green photoreceptive protein pigment that senses day length and thus controls the plant response to the duration of daylight.

Water

Plants require water for every physiological function, and in fact growth occurs only in turgid cells (cells distended with water). Most herbaceous plants are composed of 70 to 85 percent water, whereas many woody plants are composed of as much as 50 percent water. The amount of water available to plants significantly influences growth. The exact requirements are not as specifically determined as for light and temperature, but it is well known that plants will not thrive in either drought or flooded conditions.

Symptoms of too much water are similar to symptoms of low light intensity: Tissues fail to develop normally, root hairs do not develop, stems are elongated, and leaves are broad and thin. Symptoms of drought conditions are similar to symptoms of high light intensity: small and compact plants, short and stout stems, and small and thick leaves.

Timing the holiday bloom of poinsettias

Poinsettias are popularly grown for Christmas. When grown naturally, they initiate "flowers" (actually bracts) between September 25 and October 1, based on a critical day length of twelve hours, twenty minutes. Bract development continues from that point onward, as long as the day length continues to shorten and darkness is uninterrupted. Exposure to lights from nearby homes, billboards, automobiles, and streetlights can interrupt the long night requirement and thus inhibit bract development. Often in production greenhouses, black cloth is pulled over poinsettias beginning October 1 to eliminate unwanted light and guarantee fourteen hours of continuous darkness, as shown in plate 7. Under these conditions, plants are in bloom by early December, in time for the holiday season.

Too much water can be a deterrent to root growth. Shrubs planted in clay soil with poor drainage usually decline, even without the presence of root rot pathogens. If plants survive, then fungal root-rot pathogens that thrive in wet situations (such as *Pythium* and *Phytophthora*) may infect roots, as with *Rhododendron*, shown in plate 8. Roots respire and need oxygen to absorb water and minerals; therefore, they will die if they do not have access to air. Because water displaces air, too much water in the root zone can cause plants to die.

Plants that grow well in dry situations include *Phlox*, coneflower (*Rudbeckia*), *Sedum* (shown in plate 9), *Yucca*, Kentucky coffeetree (*Gymnocladus dioica*), and juniper (*Juniperus*). Plants that prefer constantly moist to wet soils include *Astilbe*, *Iris*, *Lobelia*, European alder (*Alnus glutinosa*), white willow (*Salix alba*), and redosier dogwood (*Cornus sericea*). Locating a plant that prefers dry soil, such as *Sedum*, in a wet site will lead to plant decline, possibly invasion by root rot pathogens, and plant death. Many references list the water requirements or preferences of trees, shrubs, and flowers. Try to select plants that will thrive in the conditions available on the existing site, which is much easier than trying to alter the site, particularly when there is an existing landscape design.

Temperature

Because it impacts the rate of many chemical reactions in a plant, which in turn determines the rate of growth, temperature has a significant influence on plant growth. Of course, growth and development will only occur if there is more constructive metabolism than destructive metabolism, and both are influenced by temperature.

PLANT HARDINESS ZONES. The range of temperatures in which plants can grow varies with the species and the condition of the plant. Generally, plants do not thrive when they are located more than 100 miles north or south of their native range. Although other factors, such as soil conditions, wind, and water, can be involved in plant survival out of its natural home range, temperature has the most significant impact. The U.S. Department of Agriculture (USDA) and several arboretums, all of which rate sections of the United States based on the limits of average annual minimum temperature, have developed plant hardiness ratings. These ratings provide a good idea of the cold hardiness one can expect in a specific hardiness zone, and make it possible to select plants that are likely to grow well there.

Although well-drained soil, wind protection, better fertility, and mulching will help plants survive out of their natural home range, pushing the limits of cold hardiness is not recommended. That is because a plant grown in an undesignated area often eventually succumbs to a severe winter or to the many opportunistic fungi and insects that attack stressed plants.

It is important to understand that the hardiness zones do not take into account heat tolerance. For example, the Fraser fir (*Abies fraseri*) thrives in the mountains of North Carolina where it is popular in Christmas tree plantations. Growers in Illinois would prefer to grow their own Fraser firs to meet market needs—and indeed the tree is winter hardy in zones 4 to 7 (based on Arnold Arboretum hardiness zones), covering all of Illinois. Fraser firs will survive in Illinois for a few years; however, they do not thrive there and will not produce a reliable crop. They suffer during the hot, dry summer weather common in Illinois, which results in stress that predisposes the trees to other problems. Root decline, disease, or injury from sudden temperature changes often plagues such trees during fall or winter. The problem is not cold hardiness but rather heat stress.

MINIMUM, MAXIMUM, AND OPTIMUM TEMPERATURES. There are some cardinal temperature points for plant growth. Below the minimum temperature and above the maximum temperature, no growth will occur. Temperatures in between are called optimum and are the preferred growth temperatures for the plant. The minimum, maximum, and optimum temperatures are not fixed temperatures; rather, they vary with the species, the stage of growth, and the plant part. For example, the optimum temperature for Kentucky bluegrass (*Poa pratensis*) roots is lower than for Kentucky bluegrass foliage. In the Midwest, it is best to seed a Kentucky bluegrass lawn in August. Warm temperatures allow rapid germination to give plants a good start, and the subsequent cooler temperatures of September and October favor root establishment rather than top growth. This enables plants to become established before exposed to heat stress the following summer.

Another example is the tender new growth of young plants, which is more sensitive to temperature extremes and will not tolerate cold or hot temperatures. Plate 10 shows cold injury (late spring frost) to new growth of Douglas fir (*Pseudotsuga menziesii*). Older tissue can tolerate both lower and higher temperatures and grow at them. New growth is usually most affected by late spring frosts. Plant parts even on the same tree may have a different set of cardinal temperature points. For example, as shown in plate 11, flowers of the redbud tree (*Cercis canadensis*) develop before there is any foliar (leaf) growth. The flowers begin to fade as leaves begin to grow.

HARDENING OFF. Acclimatization, or *hardening off*, is the process plants undergo to tolerate weather extremes, particularly temperature extremes. When plants are gradually exposed to lower and lower temperatures, they become hardened off. The process causes a concentration of cell sap, an increase in the percentage of bound water in tissues (which cannot readily freeze), and the formation of thickened epidermal tissue and compact internal tissues. All of these conditions occur naturally each fall and winter as a plant prepares for winter. Fertilizing plants in late summer can disrupt this process—encouraging new growth and predisposing plants to winter injury. For this reason, fertilization is usually recommended in late fall once the hardening-off process has begun and environmental conditions will not allow the development of extensive succulent new growth.

Winter injury may occur naturally when fall temperatures are mild and there is a sudden subzero temperature drop. The result is often undetected

Vernalization to induce flowering

Some seeds or seedlings—most notably winter annuals and biennials—require a period of low temperature to induce flowering when plants are mature. This process of inducing flowers is known as *vernalization*. After one season of vegetative growth, plants are exposed to winter temperatures and then flower the following spring. Foxglove (*Digitalis*) is an example of a biennial that requires vernalization. Monkshood (*Aconitum napellus*) and New York aster (*Aster novi-belgii*) are examples of perennial plants requiring annual vernalization. Without a cold period, these species will not form flowers. Spring flowering bulbs also require a period of chilling to initiate flowers. Usually this is ten to thirteen weeks of temperatures below 40° Fahrenheit (4.4° Celsius). Spring flowering bulbs are planted in the fall to flower the following spring; they will not flower the first year if planted in the spring.

until the next spring, when stem dieback and cankering are noticed. Trees experiencing other stresses, such as being out of their natural hardiness zone or in an exposed site, suffer the most damage.

In the spring, hardening off is useful for seedlings that have been grown indoors. Slowly exposing such seedlings to cooler temperatures enables them to withstand the stress of transplanting to the outdoors, where light intensity, temperature, and wind can kill tender transplants.

Inorganic salts

Nutrients are the final requirement for plant growth. It is generally agreed that seventeen elements are essential for plant growth. If an essential element is absent, then the plant will be unable to complete its life cycle, because the element is part of some essential plant constituent or metabolite. The *macronutrients*—hydrogen, carbon, oxygen, nitrogen, potassium, calcium, magnesium, phosphorous, and sulfur—are often designated as essential because they are usually involved in the structure of molecules. Hydrogen, carbon, and oxygen are supplied by water and air. The *micronutrients*—chlorine, boron, iron, manganese, zinc, copper, nickel, and molybdenum—have catalytic and regulatory roles. Micronutrients are also essential elements but are not required in large quantities by the plant.

The inorganic salts (including both macronutrients and micronutrients) absorbed by roots are dissolved in the soil solution and exist as ions rather than as individual elements. Most inorganic salts are readily available in soil or water in the landscape, and fertilization is generally needed only in situations in which drainage, soil pH, poor soils, or other stress factors limit the availability of nutrients. Signs of nutrient deficiency include stunted growth, small leaves, discoloration of foliage, and stem dieback.

Some plants will have special needs that become evident when planted on the site. For example, iron or manganese deficiency is common in high pH soils with a high concentration of clay. Pin oak, red maple (*Acer rubrum*), birch (*Betula* species), and sweetgum (*Liquidambar styraciflua*) trees frequently develop leaf chlorosis (yellowing or blanching), reduced leaf size, and early leaf drop under these conditions, as shown in plate 12. Symptoms worsen in hot, dry weather or when roots are stressed. Thus, in a landscape design, it is important to consider the limitations of the site and the nutrient stress problems common to various plants, and to make wise plant choices on the basis of this information.

Influence of stress on plant needs

Under ideal growing conditions, plant needs are met and the plant should have the ability to ward off many insect, mite, and disease problems. In reality, the ideal growing situation is unlikely ever to exist in the landscape because of ever-present environmental, site, or other plant stress factors. *Stress* is any external factor that limits the plant's growth and development. IPM involves understanding plant needs and the effects of stress factors. Table 1 lists some common sources of stress to landscape plants discussed throughout this book.

Perhaps the most important gardening decision you can make to avoid pest problems in the landscape is to select plants carefully. Cultivated varieties are carefully bred for specific horticultural design qualities such as flower color, fall color, and mature size. Often, however, the same effort has not gone into breeding for resistance to disease and insects. Wild or native plants have been bred by nature to survive; however, they do not always have the most favor-

Table 1. Common sources of stress to landscape plants

air pollution	moisture extremes (drought,
chemical injury	flooding)
diseases	nutrient imbalance
drainage problems	root injury
improper plant selection	salt applications nearby
improper planting	soil compaction
insects and mites	soil pH extremes
light problems (sun versus	temperature extremes (frost, heat)
shade)	trunk injury (scald)

able horticultural qualities. Hard-to-find information about disease and insect resistance is sometimes available through botanic gardens, plant breeders, university trials, scientific publications, and some trade magazines.

Site and environmental stress factors are probably what most significantly limit the supply of plant needs and the ability to defend against attack by insects, mites, and disease problems. In some cases, there are remedial actions that can minimize such stress factors.

Hydration stress factors

Soil drainage problems often adversely affect plant growth in the landscape. Thus, soil preparation and provisions for good soil drainage are probably second to plant selection in importance because these factors cannot be changed once plants are established. Landscapes at new home sites are often plagued by poorly drained clay subsoil, and plants in such locations are very slow to become established. The soil is frequently saturated with water after rainfall, preventing oxygen from reaching roots and resulting in root injury. Pythium and phytophthora root rots thrive under these conditions. A planting site with good drainage is an absolute must when placing plants in the landscape.

Drought stress, on the other hand, also significantly increases susceptibility of many plants to disease and insect pests. Drought-stressed pines (*Pinus*) are predisposed to infection by sphaeropsis canker and tip blight, a disease shown in plate 13. Furthermore, bark beetles, wood-boring insects, mites, and aphids are more prevalent on trees under drought stress. Although trees and shrubs should be able to withstand some drought, knowing when supplemental irrigation is needed will help you avoid severe pest problems.

Even excess or improper irrigation can cause disease problems. Pythium blight, for example, often kills large patches of lawns that are overwatered. Downy mildew (*Peronospora sparsa*) of rose (plate 14) and garden perennials is more likely to occur in gardens where frequent overhead irrigation is used. Water the soil around plants rather than the foliage whenever possible, to help prevent prolonged leaf wetting, a condition that promotes many plant diseases. Also try to water plants early in the day, so foliage will be dry by evening.

Fertilization stress factors

Horticulturalists recommend balanced fertilization that is appropriate for the specific soil type and site. Applying excessive fertilizer is a common mistake that can do much more harm than good. Overfertilization causes an abundance of succulent new growth that is more susceptible to diseases such as fire blight (*Erwinia amylovora*) of apple, crabapple, and pear. Sucking insects and mites are also known to increase in numbers when plants are overfertilized. Vascular diseases such as verticillium wilt may spread more quickly in a tree that has been heavily fertilized, possibly due to the increased size of xylem vessels. It helps to know the specific pests of concern for the particular plant and to fertilize only when symptoms and soil tests show a need.

Other stress factors

Root injury and soil compaction are common stress factors in landscape settings. Cytospora (*Leucostoma*) canker is a common disease that is known as a stress pathogen of spruce. Plate 15 shows a spruce with severe injury from this disease. Such pathogens are usually present in the landscape but do not harm plants until the plants are stressed. Avoiding root injury or compaction, especially around trees, helps to prevent infection by stress pathogens.

Finally, disease pathogens are potential stress factors for other disease problems. The repeated early season defoliation of crabapples in the spring leads to invasion by canker fungi. Chronic infection on susceptible crabapple cultivars eventually leads to plant decline and death.

IPM involves understanding the needs of the plant, the stress factors affecting the plant, and the pest problems that might be encountered. The best management practices result from considering all of these together.

Planting trees at the proper depth

Planting a tree too deeply is a common horticultural problem leading to tree decline and death. In most cases, trees in a nursery are initially planted correctly. To avoid using herbicides but still control weeds, some nurseries cultivate the soil around trees. The cultivation methods often throw soil toward the trunk. Over a few seasons, 2 to 3 inches of soil may accumulate above the original soil grade around the trunk. Trees are then dug and prepared for sale with this additional soil.

When planting nursery trees into the landscape, it is important to make certain that the first root is placed just below the soil line. To accomplish this placement, it may be necessary to remove several inches of soil from the top of the root ball before planting. Failure to do so may result in a tree that is planted too deeply, as with the spruce tree in figure 7. Because the base of the trunk is covered with soil, inadequate

Figure 7. Base of a spruce tree planted too deeply, as indicated by the branches emerging from the soil. Photo courtesy of Nancy R. Pataky

oxygen exchange occurs in the lower trunk, causing the tree to begin a slow decline. Properly planted trees exhibit a flare of the trunk as it enters the soil. The trunk of a tree that has been planted too deeply often appears to be of the same diameter all the way to the soil line, much like a telephone pole.

Plate 1. Landscape in full sun. Photo courtesy of Raymond A. Cloyd

Plate 2. Landscape in shade. Photo courtesy of Raymond A. Cloyd

Plate 3. The stem tip in the foreground shows four years of growth. The tissue between bud scale scars is the growth of one year. Photo courtesy of Nancy R. Pataky

Plate 4. Chrysanthemum with Pythium root rot, causing restricted root growth, wilted foliage, and brown leaves. Photo courtesy of Nancy R. Pataky

Plate 5. Pin oak with chlorosis in a high pH soil. Photo courtesy of Nancy R. Pataky

Plate 6. Hostas grow well in shady locations. Photo courtesy of James C. Schmidt

Plate 7. Poinsettias in a greenhouse production area. The shade cloth used to manipulate day length can be seen in the background. Photo courtesy of James C. Schmidt

Plate 8. Wilted rhododendron with Phytophthora root rot, which is common in wet, poorly drained planting areas. Photo courtesy of Donald G. White

Plate 9. *Sedum* will grow in dry locations and does well in rock gardens. Photo courtesy of James C. Schmidt

Plate 10. Injury to new spring growth of Douglas fir due to late frost. Photo courtesy of Bruce E. Paulsrud

Plate 11. Redbud tree showing flower formation before leaves emerge. Photo courtesy of James C. Schmidt

Plate 12. Nutrient stress on red maple resulting from high soil pH and low manganese availability. Photo courtesy of Nancy R. Pataky

Plate 13. Sphaeropsis blight of pine. Photo courtesy of Nancy R. Pataky

Plate 14. Downy mildew (*Peronospora sparsa*) of rose. Photo courtesy of Nancy R. Pataky

Plate 15. Severe injury on a spruce tree from stress and cytospora canker. Photo courtesy of James Schuster

Plate 16. Powdery mildew on lilac (*Syringa* species) interferes with photosynthesis but does not kill the plant. Photo courtesy of Nancy R. Pataky

Plate 17. Red osier dogwood showing symptoms of septoria leaf spot disease. Photo courtesy of Nancy R. Pataky

Plate 18. Rust spores on leaves of *Canna*. Photo courtesy of Nancy R. Pataky

Plate 19. This conk (also called shelf fungus or bracket fungus), located on a declining tree trunk, is the fruiting body of a wood rot fungus. Photo courtesy of Nancy R. Pataky

Plate 20. Anthracnose infection on oak. Photo courtesy of Nancy R. Pataky

Plate 21. Galls of crown gall bacterial disease on wintercreeper euonymus. Photo courtesy of Nancy R. Pataky

Plate 22. Bacterial leaf scorch causes decline in an oak tree. Photo courtesy of Nancy R. Pataky

Plate 23. Impatiens necrotic spot virus on impatiens plants. Photo courtesy of Donald G. White

Plate 24. Pine wilt of a mature Scotch pine tree. Photo courtesy of Nancy R. Pataky

Plate 25. Typical symptoms of foliar nematodes on hosta. Photo courtesy of Donald G. White

Plate 26. Aster yellows disease in marigolds. Photo courtesy of James Schuster

Plate 27. Mistletoe in an oak tree, as evidenced by the dark clumps of growth. Photo courtesy of Nancy R. Pataky

Plate 28. Hens and chicks infected with slime mold. Photo courtesy of Nancy R. Pataky

Plate 29. Rhizomorphs of the armillaria root rot fungus growing on a dead tree stump. Photo courtesy of Nancy R. Pataky

Plate 30. Bacterial leaf scorch on the leaves of an oak tree. Photo courtesy of Nancy R. Pataky

Plate 31. Rose mosaic virus, shown here on a rose branch, is often spread by vegetative propagation. Photo courtesy of Nancy R. Pataky

Plate 32. An example of a local infection of black spot of rose. Photo courtesy of Nancy R. Pataky

Plate 33. Botrytis blight of geranium, showing the extensive spore formation that is easily spread by wind. Photo courtesy of Donald G. White

Plate 34. Bark beetle adult covered with fungal spores on pine. Photo courtesy of Philip L. Nixon

Plate 35. Petiole blight of hosta with tan, mustard-seed-sized resting bodies called sclerotia. Photo courtesy of Nancy R. Pataky

Plate 36. Mature cedar apple rust galls on the Eastern redcedar host. Photo courtesy of Donald G. White

Plate 37. Powdery mildew of zinnia is a polycyclic disease and is primarily air disseminated. Photo courtesy of Nancy R. Pataky

Plate 38. Oak wilt is an example of a polyetic (multi–year) disease. Photo courtesy of Nancy R. Pataky

Plate 39. Ash anthracnose causes leaf spots and often causes leaf drop in the spring. Photo courtesy of Nancy R. Pataky

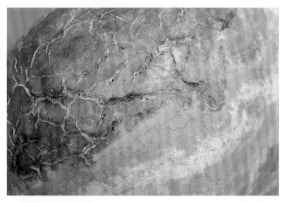

Plate 40. Water-soaked tissues caused by bacterial fruit blotch of watermelon. Photo courtesy of Nancy R. Pataky

Plate 41. Variable oakleaf caterpillar larva showing five pairs of prolegs. Photo courtesy of Philip L. Nixon

Plate 42. Introduced pine sawfly larva showing eight pairs of prolegs. Photo courtesy of Philip L. Nixon

Plate 43. Egg mass from a yellownecked caterpillar on the underside of a leaf. Photo courtesy of Philip L. Nixon

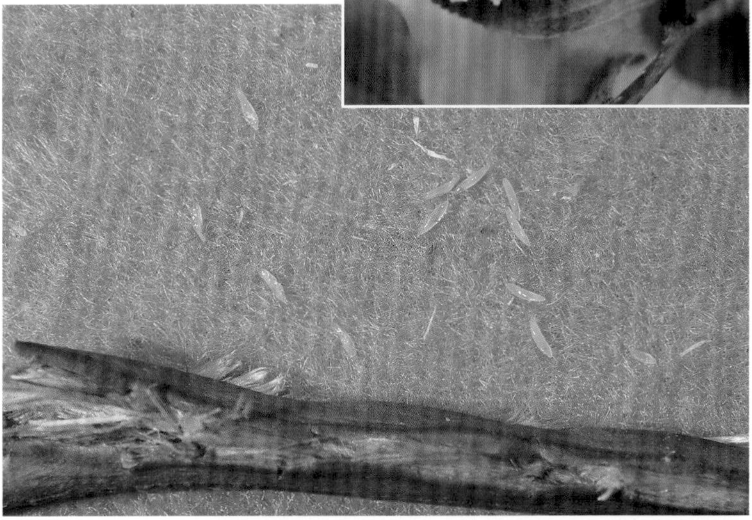

Plate 44. Periodical cicada egg-laying damage to a twig with removed eggs. Photo courtesy of Philip L. Nixon

Plate 45. Annual cicada adult in the process of molting from the nymph. Photo courtesy of Philip L. Nixon

Plate 46. Boxelder bug nymphs and adults. Photo courtesy of Philip L. Nixon

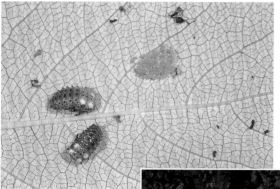

Plate 47. Cottonwood leaf beetle eggs and pupae. Photo courtesy of Philip L. Nixon

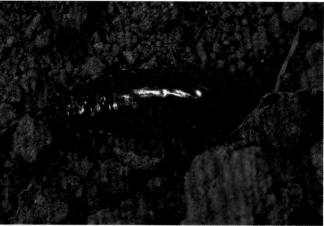

Plate 48. Cutworm pupa. Photo courtesy of Philip L. Nixon

Plate 49. Cecropia moth cocoon. Photo courtesy of Philip L. Nixon

Plate 50. Elm leaf beetle larva with associated window-feeding damage. Photo courtesy of Philip L. Nixon

Plate 51. Japanese beetle adults with associated skeletonization. Photo courtesy of Philip L. Nixon

Plate 52. Yellownecked caterpillars with associated defoliation. Photo courtesy of Philip L. Nixon

Plate 53. Honeylocust borer larva with associated cambium tunneling. Photo courtesy of Philip L. Nixon

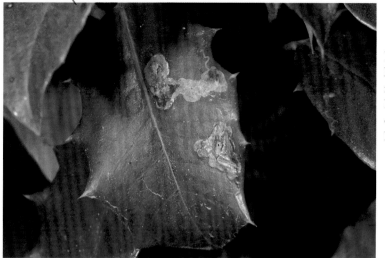

Plate 54. Holly leafminer feeding damage. Photo courtesy of Philip L. Nixon

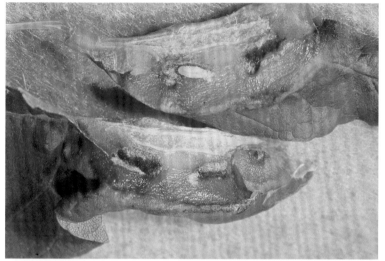

Plate 55. Ash midrib gall split open to show the gall interior and the insect larva. Photo courtesy of Philip L. Nixon

Plate 56. Twospotted spider mites with associated stippling. Photo courtesy of Philip L. Nixon

Plate 57. Aphids with associated leaf curling and distortion. Photo courtesy of Philip L. Nixon

Plate 58. White streaking on chrysanthemum flower petals caused by thrips. Photo courtesy of Philip L. Nixon

Plate 59. Gray garden slug with its mucus trail. Photo courtesy of Philip L. Nixon

Plate 60. Slug damage on hosta. Photo courtesy of Philip L. Nixon

Plate 61. Rose chafer adults feeding on a rose flower. Photo courtesy of Raymond A. Cloyd

Plate 62. Japanese beetle adults feeding on a marigold flower. Photo courtesy of Raymond A. Cloyd

Plate 63. Tomato hornworm caterpillar. Photo courtesy of Raymond A. Cloyd

Plate 64. Grasshopper adult feeding on a leaf. Photo courtesy of Raymond A. Cloyd

Plate 65. Earwig adult. Photo courtesy of Raymond A. Cloyd

Plate 66. Weevil adult. Photo courtesy of Raymond A. Cloyd

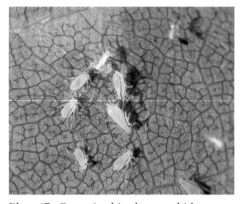

Plate 67. Green in this photo, aphids vary in color from green, orange, to black depending on the food source. Photo courtesy of Raymond A. Cloyd

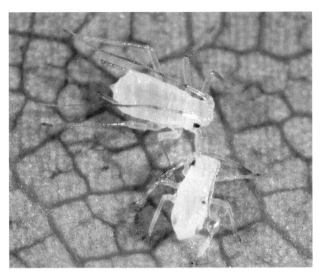

Plate 68. Aphids. Notice tubes on abdomen, called *cornicles*. Photo courtesy of Raymond A. Cloyd

Plate 69. Aphid feeding on a leaf. Its piercing-sucking mouthparts enable it to withdraw plant fluids. Photo courtesy of Raymond A. Cloyd

Plate 70. Whitefly adults on leaf underside. Photo courtesy of Raymond A. Cloyd

Plate 71. Whitefly adult. Photo courtesy of Raymond A. Cloyd

Plate 72. Immature whiteflies on leaf underside. Their piercing-sucking mouthparts enable them to withdraw plant fluids. Photo courtesy of Raymond A. Cloyd

Plate 73. Both adult and immature stages of citrus mealybug. Photo courtesy of Raymond A. Cloyd

Plate 74. Oystershell scale on red osier dogwood. Photo courtesy of Raymond A. Cloyd

Plate 75. Wax scale on holly. Photo courtesy of Raymond A. Cloyd

Plate 76. Leafhopper adult. Photo courtesy of Raymond A. Cloyd

Plate 77. Twospotted spider mite adult. Photo courtesy of Raymond A. Cloyd

Plate 78. Impatiens necrotic spot virus on impatiens. Ringspots are characteristic of many viruses. Photo courtesy of Raymond A. Cloyd

Plate 79. Columbine leaf damaged from leafminer tunneling. Photo courtesy of Raymond A. Cloyd

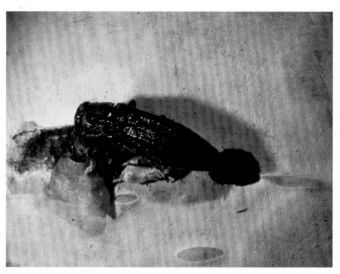

Plate 80. Bronze birch borer adult emerging from a birch tree. Photo courtesy of John Davidson

Plate 81. Wood-boring insect larvae and associated tunneling damage to a young cedar. Photo courtesy of Raymond A. Cloyd

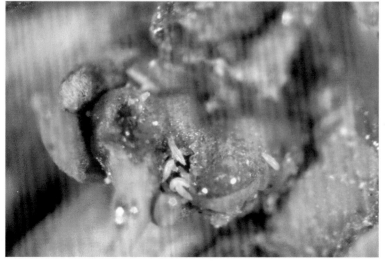

Plate 82. Eriophyid mites in the terminal growth of a juniper. Photo courtesy of Raymond A. Cloyd

Plate 83. Maple bladder gall caused by an eriophyid mite. Photo courtesy of Raymond A. Cloyd

Plate 84. Ash flower gall caused by an eriophyid mite. Photo courtesy of Raymond A. Cloyd

Plate 85. Hackberry nipple gall-maker caused by a psyllid. Photo courtesy of Raymond A. Cloyd

Plate 86. Heavy infestation of cypress twig gall midge (*Taxodiomyia cupressiananassa*). Photo courtesy of Raymond A. Cloyd

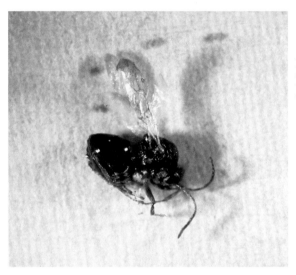

Plate 87. Cynipid gall wasp adult. Photo courtesy of Raymond A. Cloyd

Plate 88. Galls on oak tree caused by a cynipid gall wasp. Photo courtesy of Raymond A. Cloyd

Plate 89. Aphids feeding on terminal growth, where they are exposed to natural enemies. Photo courtesy of Raymond A. Cloyd

Plate 90. Parasitized aphids (gray-brown colored aphids) on a leaf. Photo courtesy of Raymond A. Cloyd

Plate 91. Leafminer larvae tunneling in verbena leaf. Photo courtesy of Raymond A. Cloyd

Plate 92. Molting skin of an insect. Photo courtesy of Raymond A. Cloyd

Plate 93. Aphid molting cast skins on a citrus leaf, which may be mistaken for whiteflies without close observation. Photo courtesy of Raymond A. Cloyd

Plate 94. Honeydew (a by-product of insects with piercing-sucking mouthparts) on a ficus leaf. Photo courtesy of Raymond A. Cloyd

Plate 95. Black sooty mold fungus on southern yew. Photo courtesy of Raymond A. Cloyd

Plate 96. Gypsy moth larva or caterpillar. Photo courtesy of Clifford S. Sadof

Plate 97. Dark black fecal deposits are a by-product of lace bug feeding. Photo courtesy of Raymond A. Cloyd

Plate 98. Grubs feeding on turf. Photo courtesy of Philip L. Nixon

Plate 99. Colony of eastern tent caterpillar on a crabapple tree. Photo courtesy of Raymond A. Cloyd

Plate 100. Eastern tent caterpillar, one of the early defoliators, on nest. Photo courtesy of Raymond A. Cloyd

Plate 101. Fall webworm caterpillars remain in their nest while feeding. Photo courtesy of Clifford S. Sadof

Plate 102. Fall webworm caterpillars. Second-generation fall webworm caterpillars are of less concern because they feed on trees late in the season. Photo courtesy of Raymond A. Cloyd

Plate 103. Red maple with verticillium wilt. Photo courtesy of Philip L. Nixon

Plate 104. Larger sod webworm larva. Photo courtesy of Philip L. Nixon

Plate 105. Leaf damage on snap beans caused by bean leaf beetle adults. Photo courtesy of Philip L. Nixon

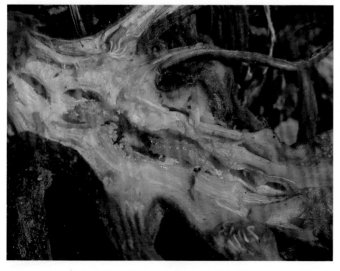

Plate 106. Squash vine borer damage. Photo courtesy of Philip L. Nixon

Plate 107. Iris borer larvae feeding on tall bearded iris. Photo courtesy of Philip L. Nixon

Plate 108. Dandelions competing with tall grass. Photo courtesy of Philip L. Nixon

Plate 109. Linden borer larvae and damage to a tree stressed by transplanting and being planted too deeply. Photo courtesy of Philip L. Nixon

Plate 110. A properly mulched tree in a landscape. Photo courtesy of Philip L. Nixon

Plate 111. Sweetgum with chlorosis. Photo courtesy of Raymond A. Cloyd

Plate 112. Potato leafhopper damage on potato foliage. Photo courtesy of Philip L. Nixon

Plate 113. Carpetweed growing in compacted soil. Photo courtesy of Philip L. Nixon

Plate 114. Conks (fruiting bodies) of wood rot fungi. Photo courtesy of Philip L. Nixon

Plate 115. Oozing sap due to fire blight. Photo courtesy of Philip L. Nixon

Plate 116. Japanese beetle adults feeding on rose blossoms. Photo courtesy of Philip L. Nixon

Plate 117. Strawberry root weevil adult and associated damage to rose blossom. Photo courtesy of Philip L. Nixon

Plate 118. Removing bagworms by handpicking. Photo courtesy of Philip L. Nixon

Plate 119. Eastern tent caterpillar egg mass. Photo courtesy of Philip L. Nixon

Plate 120. Squash bug egg mass. Photo courtesy of Philip L. Nixon

Plate 121. A high population of Japanese beetle adults feeding on a linden tree. Photo courtesy of Raymond A. Cloyd

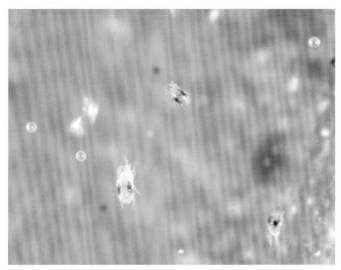

Plate 122. Twospotted spider mites. Photo courtesy of Raymond A. Cloyd

Plate 123. Twospotted spider mite damage to burning bush (*Euonymus alatus*). Photo courtesy of Raymond A. Cloyd

Plate 124. Pine needle scale on mugo pine. Photo courtesy of Raymond A. Cloyd

Plate 125. Certain predatory bugs feed on a plant as a supplemental food source, which may increase the risk of exposure to systemic insecticides. Photo courtesy of Raymond A. Cloyd

Plate 126. Parasitoid: *Leptomastix dactylopii* is a parasitoid of citrus mealybug. Photo courtesy of Raymond A. Cloyd

Plate 127. Predator: minute pirate bug (*Orius tristicolor*) is a predator of thrips, aphids, and spider mites. Photo courtesy of Raymond A. Cloyd

Plate 128. Pathogen: caterpillar infected with a fungus. Photo courtesy of Raymond A. Cloyd

Plate 129. Parasitized aphids (gray-brown) on a leaf. Photo courtesy of Raymond A. Cloyd

Plate 130. Adult parasitoid emerging from a dead (parasitized) aphid. Photo courtesy of Raymond A. Cloyd

Plate 131. Parasitoid emergence holes in scales that had been parasitized. Photo courtesy of Raymond A. Cloyd

Plate 132. Parasitoid cocoons on a caterpillar. Photo courtesy of Raymond A. Cloyd

Plate 133. Beneficial nematodes. Photo courtesy of Raymond A. Cloyd

Plate 134. Ladybird beetle larvae eating a cottony cushion scale. Photo courtesy of Raymond A. Cloyd

Plate 135. Praying mantis (mantid) adult. Photo courtesy of Raymond A. Cloyd

Plate 136. Praying mantis (mantid) egg case. Photo courtesy of Raymond A. Cloyd

Plate 137. Predator: ground beetle. Photo courtesy of Raymond A. Cloyd

Plate 138. Predator: ladybird beetle adult. Photo courtesy of Raymond A. Cloyd

Plate 139. Predator: ladybird beetle larvae. Photo courtesy of Raymond A. Cloyd

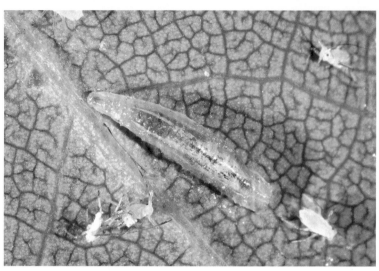

Plate 140. Predator: hover fly (syrphid fly) larvae feeding on aphids. Photo courtesy of Raymond A. Cloyd

Plate 141. Predator: green lacewing eggs on leaf. Photo courtesy of Raymond A. Cloyd

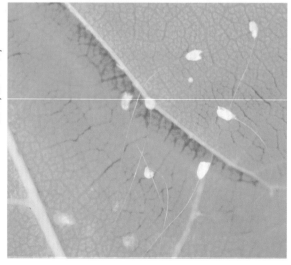

Plate 142. Predator: close up of green lacewing eggs on stalks. This prevents siblings from eating each other. Photo courtesy of Raymond A. Cloyd

Plate 143. Predator: green lacewing larvae eating an aphid. Photo courtesy of Raymond A. Cloyd

Plate 144. Predator: green lacewing adult. Adults primarily feed on pollen and nectar. Photo courtesy of Clifford S. Sadof

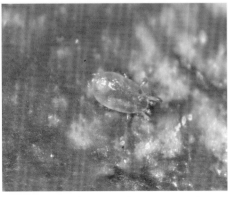

Plate 145. Predator: predatory mite. Photo courtesy of Raymond A. Cloyd

Plate 146. Predator: minute pirate bug adult. Photo courtesy of Raymond A. Cloyd

Plate 147. Ants tending scale. Ants protect sucking insects such as scale from natural enemies. Photo courtesy of Raymond A. Cloyd

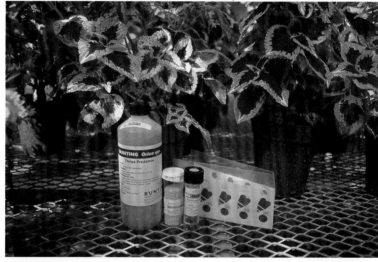

Plate 148. Containers of biological control agents that can be purchased from suppliers. Photo courtesy of Raymond A. Cloyd

Plate 149. Container of ladybird beetle adults. Photo courtesy of Raymond A. Cloyd

Chapter 2

Disease Needs

Integrated pest management uses a variety of strategies to reduce plant pests. Disease pathogens comprise one group of plant pests. This chapter discusses:

- conditions favorable to plant pathogens
- conditions necessary for a disease to develop
- mechanisms of attack that disease pathogens use
- plant responses to pathogens

A healthy plant exhibits normal growth, differentiation, and development when all of its physiological functions are working well. These functions include absorption and translocation (movement) of water and minerals, photosynthesis, translocation of plant products, metabolism of plant components, reproduction, and storage. All plant functions are interrelated, in that each depends on the others to keep the plant healthy. When plant health is disturbed by the continual irritation of a pathogen or environmental conditions, the plant becomes diseased.

Plant diseases interfere with one or more plant functions. The result is weakened or destroyed plant cells or tissues, reduced growth, and sometimes plant death. Which physiological function is affected first depends on the site of infection. Thus a root rot may interfere with root absorption; a wilt disease may affect the xylem and translocation of water and nutrients; and a leaf pathogen (such as powdery mildew, shown in plate 16) may affect photo-

33

synthesis. If actions are not taken to help the plant, then other physiological functions may also be affected, leading to decline. If a plant continues to decline in health, it will likely die.

Understanding plant disease

In most cases, *plant disease* is the impairment of the normal appearance or functions of a plant caused by a pathogenic agent. Sometimes an environmental irritant is causative. *Plant symptoms* are the visible indicators of disease that result from the continual irritation by the causal agent or environmental stress over time. Symptoms are descriptions of plant appearance, such as chlorotic (yellowed), blighted (tissue death), and spotted. *Septoria cornicola*, an example of leaf spot, is shown in plate 17. Disease is different from injury, which happens quickly, if not instantaneously—such as from a lightning strike.

As with human diseases, plant diseases may be infectious or noninfectious. Diseases caused by a biotic (living) agent, or by an agent that can grow and multiply, are *infectious*. Diseases caused by abiotic (nonliving) agents, such as environmental stress, are *noninfectious*. Possible causes of noninfectious disease include

- temperature extremes
- too much or too little moisture
- light extremes
- lack of oxygen
- air pollution
- nutrient imbalances
- pH imbalance
- pesticide toxicity
- improper cultural practices

Iron chlorosis of pin oak or sweetgum trees is an example of a noninfectious disease. It develops in areas where the soil pH is alkaline, causing iron to be tied up in the soil and unavailable to the plant roots. Over a few years, the foliage becomes progressively chlorotic and growth is reduced. If the condition is untreated, branch decline becomes evident (death of branch tips and fewer, small, and off-color leaves), followed by early death of the tree. It is essential to determine whether the disease is infectious or noninfectious to manage the problem effectively. For example, using a fungicide or removing the affected branches would not help a tree suffering from iron chlorosis. Altering soil pH or injecting the tree with an available form of iron would be more effective.

The disease triangle and pyramid

The appearance of an infectious plant disease depends on three factors, often referred to as the *disease triangle*. The three factors necessary are a virulent pathogen, a susceptible host, and an environment conducive to development of the pathogen; and each side of the triangle represents a factor. The length of the sides is sometimes used to represent the proportion of each factor, and in that case, the area within the triangle represents the amount of disease present. The triangle illustrates that the factors are interrelated in the disease process. If one side of the triangle is missing, then there is no area within the triangle, and disease is absent.

Because the disease process also has an assumed function of time, it is often depicted as a pyramid, with time as the fourth side of the polyhedron, as shown in figure 8. The disease pyramid is a simplified symbol, but it relates directly to IPM of diseases. Because all of these factors are essential for a disease to occur, eliminating, altering, or reducing one factor will help to alleviate or eliminate the disease.

As we might expect, in nature it is possible for more than one pathogen to infect a plant at a time—a condition called a *disease complex*. This is impor-

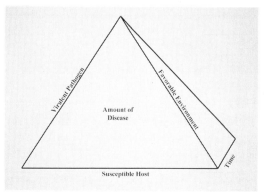

Figure 8. The disease pyramid depicts the factors that interact in a plant disease situation. Illustration by Nancy R. Pataky

tant in terms of disease management because all aspects of the complex must be considered. Ash decline is an example of a disease complex caused by both abiotic and biotic factors. Merely managing water stress, which is one of the contributing abiotic causes, will not control the disease. Sooty blotch (a complex of three fungi: *Peltaster fructicola*, *Geastrumia polystigmatis*, and *Leptodontium elatius*) and fly speck (*Schizothyrium pomi*) are two diseases that form a disease complex on apple fruit. Sooty molds, found on many landscape trees, are part of a disease complex involving the sooty mold fungus, which grows on honeydew (a clear, sticky liquid excreted by sucking insect pests). IPM relies on identifying all factors that contribute to the problem.

Plant pathogens

A living, or biotic, agent that is capable of causing disease in a plant host is called a *plant pathogen*. The agent grows and multiplies in the host plant, and it may spread to cause disease in other plants. Thus pathogens are causal agents of infectious plant disease. *Pathogenicity* is the ability of the plant parasite to interfere with physiological functions of the plant and cause disease.

Diseases may be classified according to the

- type of host infected (annuals, woody ornamentals, turfgrass)
- part of the plant affected (foliage, stem, roots)
- symptom produced (leaf spot, blight, wilt)
- causative pathogen

Disease or disorder?

Abiotic agents of disease are not considered pathogens because they cannot persist in the host and increase in numbers. A common argument is that abiotic agents do not cause plant disease. *Disorder* might serve as an alternate term for *abiotic disease*. Regardless of terminology, it is important to distinguish between biotic and abiotic causes to manage the problem effectively.

One of the more useful and common classifications of disease is by type of plant pathogen causing the disease. Plant pathogens include fungi, bacteria, viruses, nematodes, phytoplasmas, parasitic seed plants, viroids, and protozoa. By understanding something about each pathogen, we can begin to understand why diseases occur. IPM uses this information to reduce or eliminate pathogen populations and disease.

Fungi

These small, thread-like organisms with cell walls produce spores and lack chlorophyll. Fungi are responsible for the greatest number of infectious plant diseases in the landscape. They are also the largest, most highly visible, and easiest causative organisms to see. In fact, it is possible to see many fungi with the naked eye, as with the vegetative stage (mycelium) of wood rot fungi, which is visible as a white, threadlike growth on rotted wood. Mycelium may not be as visible in the high-maintenance home landscape because dead plant material is usually removed quickly.

The reproductive stage of fungi consists of spores, often in fruiting bodies of some sort. Most spores are not visible to the naked eye, but a few fungi involved in diseases, such as rust (as shown on leaves of *Canna* in plate 18), smut, and powdery mildew, form visible spores. Sometimes mushrooms (fruiting bodies) of root rot pathogens will grow on the soil around infected trees, and conks (fruiting bodies that grow only on wood) also will grow on the exterior of trunks of trees harboring wood rot, as shown in plate 19. Other fungal pathogens are visible with a hand lens, dissecting microscope, compound microscope, or possibly electron microscope.

Fungi that cause plant disease cannot use light to produce food. Because they cannot photosynthesize, they are parasitic on the plant host or use the plant as a food source. Fungal needs include a source of plant food, oxygen, and a moist location. Fungal pathogens are generally susceptible to drying and grow best in dark, wet locations. Most fungal pathogens are temperature adapted but grow best from 68° to 86° Fahrenheit (20° to 30° Celsius).

Conditions that favor the fungus usually favor disease development as well. Trees growing in shady, closely planted settings are more susceptible to foliar diseases such as anthracnose (*Discula*, as shown in plate 20) and powdery mildew than a tree planted as an individual specimen in an exposed setting.

Fungal-like organisms

Recent research on fungal differences has led to some changes in fungal taxonomy. Mycologists have moved a group of pathogens previously classified as fungal oomycetes out of the fungal kingdom (Kingdom Fungi) and into the kingdom of fungal-like organisms (Kingdom Chromista). These pathogens are still oomycetes but technically not true fungi. Plant pathogens in this kingdom include species of *Peronospora* (downy mildew) and *Pythium* and *Phytophthora* (common root rot pathogens in wet soils). Although most plant pathologists currently use fungal-like to describe these pathogens, in this book we have grouped them with the fungi.

Bacteria

Bacterial plant pathogens are microscopic and usually single-celled organisms that lack chlorophyll and must rely on a plant as a food source. They have a cell wall but do not have a nucleus. They reproduce by *fission*, which is the splitting of each bacterial cell to make two new cells. There is no sexual stage of bacterial reproduction. A few examples of plant diseases that bacteria cause include fire blight (*Erwinia amylovora*), crown gall (*Agrobacterium tumefaciens*)—shown on wintercreeper euonymus (*Euonymus fortunei*) in plate 21—lilac bacterial blight (*Pseudomonas syringae*), and bacterial leaf scorch (*Xylella fastidiosa*).

Often bacteria are visible en masse as a bacterial exudate (ooze), but individual bacterial cells are visible only with a compound microscope. Bacteria can be difficult to detect because they can be present in the plant in an inactive stage until environmental conditions are favorable. Still, the outward expression of symptoms can be quite rapid once the bacterium becomes active. Bacteria can rapidly multiply to form large populations in as little as two days.

Some plant pathogenic bacteria are specialized and are still not well understood. One such group that attacks trees in the landscape is called the *fastidious bacteria*, so named because its growth is limited to the xylem or phloem. Fastidious bacteria disrupt vascular conducting tissues. A major landscape disease caused by a member of this group of fungi is called bacterial leaf scorch, caused by *Xylella fastidiosa*. Scorch symptoms, as shown in an oak tree in plate 22, and eventual death of the tree may result from infection by this bacterium.

Viruses

Viruses are submicroscopic—too small to be seen with a compound microscope. Virus particles have no cell wall, cytoplasm, nor nucleus, so they depend on the plant to multiply. Viruses contain genetic material—nucleic acid in the form of deoxyribonucleic acid (DNA) or ribonucleic acid (RNA)—with a protein coat. Viruses can enter a plant only through wounds or by way of vectors that place them in the plant. There are many vectors of plant viruses —including seed, pollen, vegetative propagation, mites, nematodes, fungi, and even parasitic seed plants such as dodder (*Cuscuta* species)—but by far, most vectors are insects.

Once inside a cell, the virus causes the plant to produce more virus particles. In this sense, the virus uses the plant to reproduce. This process prohibits plant cells from functioning normally, and the infected plants often appear distorted or stunted, or have odd color patterns. A few common landscape virus problems include ash ringspot (tobacco ringspot and tobacco mosaic virus), impatiens necrotic spot virus (tospovirus) (shown in plate 23), and rose mosaic virus (apple mosaic virus and prunus necrotic ringspot virus).

Nematodes

These microscopic and mostly wormlike animals are more primitive than earthworms and are involved in diseases of humans and plants. Only about 10 percent of them are plant pathogens. Plant parasitic nematodes have a strong stylet (piercing mouthpart) that penetrates the plant tissue and feeds on cell contents. There are three main classifications of nematodes:

- Ectoparasitic nematodes feed on the tissues from outside the plant. Examples include ring nematodes (*Criconemella*), stunt nematodes (*Tylenchorhynchus*), and dagger nematodes (*Xiphinema*).
- Endoparasitic nematodes feed from within the plant. Examples include lesion nematodes (*Pratylenchus*), root knot nematodes (*Meloidogyne*), and the pinewood nematode (*Bursaphelenchus xylophilus*).

- Migratory nematodes move freely through the soil or plant tissue. The foliar nematode (*Aphelenchoides fragariae*) is a migratory type that can feed on or in plant tissues.

It is important to know the type of nematode feeding when attempting to control these pathogens. For example, the endoparasitic nematodes are often protected within the root from the effects of pesticides and microorganisms in the soil. Migratory types often require more than one management method. Measures taken to prevent nematode-infested plants from entering a nursery or planting might include modified watering practices to avoid wetting the foliage, as well as the use of systemic nematicides (pesticides specifically for controlling nematodes). There is no single management tool that will control migratory nematodes.

Plant nematode problems may be of greater concern in warm climates where the nematode can easily overwinter, but cooler climates have landscape nematode problems as well. Pine wilt, caused by the pinewood nematode (*Bursaphelenchus xylophilus*), can kill a mature pine in the Midwest in one summer. Plate 24 shows a 50-year-old Scotch pine (*Pinus sylvestris*) with pine wilt. Foliar nematodes are a problem on hostas, as shown in plate 25, and other garden perennials throughout the United States. In fact, root knot nematodes are probably the most damaging nematodes to woody ornamental plants in this country.

Phytoplasmas

Formerly called mycoplasma-like diseases because of the pathogen's close resemblance to mycoplasmas, phytoplasma diseases make up a comparatively small percentage of the diseases in landscape plants. However, some phytoplasma diseases can be very severe. Phytoplasmas resemble bacteria but are much larger and lack a cell wall. They have a plasma membrane, cytoplasm, and strands of DNA. Phytoplasmas colonize the phloem of plants where they reproduce by fission (simple division). Phytoplasmas often produce symptoms similar to those produced by viruses. Many diseases now known to be caused by phytoplasmas were mistakenly attributed to viruses. Examples of phytoplasma diseases in the landscape include elm phloem necrosis (elm yellows), lilac witches' broom, aster yellows, walnut and pecan bunch, and ash yellows, which is shown in marigolds in plate 26.

Parasitic seed plants

Although they are often able to provide food through photosynthesis, parasitic seed plants lack a normal root system and are parasitic on the host plant for water and nutrients. These plants do cause a few landscape disease problems: They sink modified stems (haustoria and sinkers) into the host tissue and absorb water and nutrients from the host. Dwarf mistletoes (*Arceuthobium*) and leafy mistletoes (*Phoradendron*), as shown growing in an oak tree in plate 27, broomrape (*Orobanche*), and dodder comprise most of this group of landscape pathogens.

Viroids and protozoa

These cause few diseases of plants, and none serious to landscape plants. A *viroid* is similar to a virus but much smaller; it is a circular, single-stranded RNA molecule without a protein coat. The best-known viroid disease is probably potato spindle tuber, but viroids are also responsible for chrysanthemum stunt and tomato bunchy-top. More than two dozen viroids are thought to cause plant disease, but most do not affect landscape plants.

Protozoa are mostly single-celled, microscopic animals. They move by structures such as flagella, pseudopodia, cilia, or by movements of the cell itself. Those implicated in disease are the flagellate protozoa, which only damage non-landscape plants, such as potato, coffee, and coconut plants. Slime molds, shown on hens and chicks (*Sempervivum*) in plate 28, are protozoa that do occur in landscapes but do not harm plants. These organisms are *saprophytes*, meaning that they obtain food from dead plant material. It is interesting that some protozoa feed on root pathogens, thereby reducing plant disease; these are discussed in chapter 8.

The parasitic nature of plant pathogens

Plant pathogens are parasitic on the host plant. They remove food and water from the plant cells in order to grow and multiply. In most diseases, the pathogen has an *additive effect*, meaning that the amount of damage caused to the plant is often greater than what one might expect from the loss of the water and nutrients alone. The pathogen interferes with plant physiological functions, causing increased plant damage.

When discussing pathogen needs, it is important to understand how parasites are categorized, because these categories provide clues as to how the pathogen might survive and therefore how best to manage it. Parasites are classified according to whether the food source is living, dead, or a combination of both.

OBLIGATE PARASITES. These can grow and reproduce in nature only on a living host. Rusts, powdery and downy mildews, viruses, and nematodes are obligate parasites. These pathogens may be able to survive without a host, but they will not continue to grow and reproduce without a host plant.

NONOBLIGATE PARASITES. These can grow and reproduce on either living or dead hosts. Most of the fungal and bacterial pathogens of plants are nonobligate parasites. Because of this quality, it is possible to culture most of the plant pathogenic fungi and bacteria on artificial media—a common method of confirming disease diagnosis in the laboratory.

FACULTATIVE PARASITES. These are usually saprophytes but can live as parasites as well. Anthracnose fungi are examples of this type of parasite. The facultative parasites can survive away from the host in an overwintering or oversummering survival structure—usually a mass of mycelium, a fruiting body, or a mass of dark-walled cells. Examples include the

- microsclerotia (cells that serve as a means of long-term survival of some fungi) of *Verticillium dahliae*, the cause of verticillium wilt
- rhizomorphs (root-like structures produced by a fungus) of *Armillaria mellea*, the cause of armillaria root rot, shown in plate 29
- sclerotia (resting stage of this fungus) of *Sclerotium rolfsii*, the cause of southern blight

Controlling the disease cycle through integrated pest management

The *disease cycle*—the progressive steps in the development of an infectious plant disease—involves the changes that occur in the plant as well as the changes that occur in the pathogen. IPM works to control the major events in the disease cycle and thereby limit disease occurrence and spread. The major events in a disease cycle are

- inoculation, or contact
- penetration, or entry
- establishment of infection
- dissemination of the pathogen
- survival of the pathogen without the host

Inoculation

The initial contact of the pathogen with the plant host is called *inoculation*. Research plant pathologists routinely inoculate plants with pathogens to cause disease on the host plant for further study. Artificial methods vary but are designed to mimic the natural process of inoculation. For example, a spore suspension might be flooded over a leaf surface; roots might be soaked in a spore suspension before planting; or nematodes might be injected into the soil around a root system. The *inoculum*, which is any part of the pathogen that can initiate infection, might consist of spores, mycelium, nematodes, and/or virus particles. Each unit of inoculum, such as each spore, is called a *propagule*.

Determining the source of inoculum might provide some ideas about how to prevent a disease or its spread. The inoculum for a disease pathogen may already be present on the host site or may be brought to the site. In a landscape setting, it may be in the soil (for example, microsclerotia of *Verticillium*), on plant debris (mycelia and spores of apple scab, *Venturia inaequalis*), on the host (fruiting bodies of sphaeropsis tip blight, *Sphaeropsis sapinea,* as in figure 9), or on other crops or weeds (alternate hosts of rust). In addition, it could be brought in on new plant material (rust on a daylily, *Puccinia hemerocallis*), moved by wind from nearby plants (spores of white pine blister rust), or introduced on soil or equipment (soil nematodes).

Most pathogens make contact with the plant as a matter of chance. For example, rust galls produce thousands of spores, which the wind blows to surrounding plants, covering many plant species where they cannot penetrate the epidermis or where conditions are not conducive to disease development. However, by chance they may land on a susceptible host and cause disease. Wind, water, and insects are primarily responsible for the passive

Figure 9. The fungal inoculum for sphaeropsis blight of pine may overwinter on the cones. Photo courtesy of Nancy R. Pataky

spread of inoculum. Active means of spread include some insect/animal vectors, *Pythium* and *Phytophthora* zoospores swimming to root exudates, and nematodes attracted to sugars and amino acids that diffuse from roots.

Penetration

Once inoculum is present on the plant, it must find a way to enter the plant and begin the infection process. Penetration might be directly through plant tissues, through natural openings, or through wounds. Wound entry is probably least understood, and yet this is a site that often can be controlled. A single nail driven into a tree can provide a wound for entry by damaging disease pathogens. Stubs of branches can provide a site for the entry of canker diseases and wood rot fungi. Mower or weed trimmer injury at the base of trees can allow entry of root and collar rot fungi, resulting in tree death.

With most diseases, the pathogen can enter the plant in more than one way; therefore, effective disease control hinges on being aware of all possibilities. The fire blight bacterium, *Erwinia amylovora*, may be brought to the plant on insects, in water, or by wind. It can enter the plant through wounds or natural plant openings. Disinfecting pruning tools between cuts of diseased plant material will help prevent spread of the pathogen but, because of other possible means of pathogen penetration, will not eliminate it.

Fungi most commonly enter the plant by direct penetration of the cuticle and cell wall. Sometimes, as in the case of apple scab and black spot of rose (*Diplocarpon rosae*), the fungus penetrates only the cuticle and stays between the cuticle and cell wall. Many fungi also enter the plant through natural openings and wounds.

Bacterial plant pathogens are not capable of directly penetrating plants. They often enter through natural openings such as:

Stomata. Tiny openings in the continuous network of cells that make up the epidermis

Hydathodes (water pores). Structures that secrete water droplets from within the leaf

Nectarthodes (nectaries). Structures primarily in flowers that secrete a sugary solution

Lenticels. Areas of loosely arranged cells on stems, roots, or fruit, which appear as dots on stems and are thought to function in gas exchange

The fire blight bacterium is splashed, blown, or deposited on the flowers of crabapples by bees and other insects, gaining entry into the plant via nectarthodes. Alternatively, because bacteria are usually present on plants as normal contaminants, they are readily available to enter the plant through wounds as they occur. Often an insect vector of the bacterium causes these wounds, as is the case with leafhopper transmission of the bacterial leaf scorch pathogen to oaks and other landscape trees. Plate 30 shows bacterial leaf scorch on the leaves of an oak tree.

Nematodes usually enter a plant by direct penetration through the roots. Root lesion nematodes (Pratylenchus) repeatedly use their needle-like stylets to pierce the root and then feed on injured cells or penetrate the plant. Some nematodes also enter through natural openings provided they have a film of water in which to move. The foliar nematode of hosta and other perennials will move from the crown and along the leaf surface to enter the plant via stomata.

Virus particles must be placed in the plant host because they cannot gain access on their own. Generally it is the insect or mite vector that injects viruses into plant sap during the feeding process. For example, tomato spotted wilt virus is spread by certain species of thrips (Frankliniella), and the pathogen is introduced via wounds. Some viruses and all viroids can enter the plant via wounds. Viruses also can be transmitted by vegetative propagation of buds, scions (grafted plant parts), or rootstock, as is the case with rose mosaic virus (shown in plate 31).

Phytoplasmas also enter plants via wounds made by the vector. Ash yellows is a phytoplasma disease believed to be spread by leafhoppers and certain spittlebugs.

Parasitic seed plants always enter the plant by direct penetration of plant tissues. They use outgrowths of the stem (haustoria) to penetrate and enter the plant. Special adaptations called sinkers extend into the xylem and phloem tissue of the host to obtain water and nutrients.

Establishment of infection

Infection is established when the pathogen makes contact with the susceptible cells or tissue of the plant and begins to grow and multiply. At this point, the pathogen is removing nutrients from the plant and disrupting plant functions. Symptoms might be expressed immediately, but more often the symptoms appear after two to four days. Latent infections may not be evident for weeks. This is important because infection with the pathogen may have taken place before control options were initiated.

During the infection process, the pathogen releases a number of substances such as enzymes, toxins, and growth regulators that may inhibit plant functions. The plant responds with defense mechanisms, which are discussed in chapter 5.

Pathogens may invade within cells (intracellular), between cells (intercellular), and within xylem and phloem vessels. *Local infection* involves a small area of the plant, as is the case with most fungi, bacteria, nematodes, and parasitic seed plants. Although the affected tissue remains small, multiple infection points may give the plant the appearance of a systemic infection. Local infection is spread externally. Plate 32 shows a local infection of black spot of rose.

Contact does not always equal infection

Not all pathogen-to-plant contacts will cause infection and disease. Remember that much of this contact is purely by chance. Successful infection relies on a host that is susceptible to the particular pathogen, a pathogen that is in a virulent (disease-causing) stage, and temperature and moisture conditions that will favor pathogen growth.

Systemic infection involves spread of the pathogen throughout most susceptible plant tissues by way of the vascular system (xylem and phloem). Examples include phytoplasma diseases such as ash yellows and aster yellows, most viruses, and most viroid diseases.

The final step in the establishment of infection is pathogen reproduction:

- Fungi produce spores.
- Parasitic higher plants produce seeds.
- Bacteria, phytoplasmas, and protozoa reproduce by fission (simple division).
- Viruses and viroids are replicated by the plant cell.
- Nematodes produce eggs.

Dissemination of the pathogen

Plant pathogens can move from plant to plant in several ways. This movement is not a purposeful event; rather, nearly all dissemination of plant pathogens is passive and occurs by air, water, insects, and animals (including humans). Airborne fungal spores can travel a couple of miles, but most are too fragile to go farther. The white pine blister rust fungus (*Cronartium ribicola*) usually spreads from an infected pine to a healthy pine within a few hundred yards, but it may spread farther in air streams. Spores land everywhere, not just on a susceptible host.

Wind can move seeds of parasitic seed plants, but usually for only short distances. Birds ingest berries and pass the seeds. As a result, birds may be responsible for more long-distance spread of parasitic seed plants. Diseases that produce dry spores—for example, botrytis blight of flowers (*Botrytis cinerea*), shown on geraniums in plate 33—can rely on wind dispersal for many new infections.

Water is another major method of pathogen dissemination. Soil water may carry bacteria, nematodes, spores, sclerotia, and mycelial fragments, making it a common means of pathogen and disease spread. Rain and irrigation water can spread spores, such as apple scab; and bacteria, such as fire blight. Some spores, such as those of anthracnose diseases, are produced in a slimy matrix, which aids dispersal.

Vectors are organisms that transmit pathogens. Insects, mites, and nematodes are all primary vectors of plant disease, but insects such as aphids, whiteflies, thrips, and leafhoppers transmit most viruses. In addition, leafhoppers are major vectors of phtyoplasmas and fastidious bacteria. Both pathogen groups also can spread by vegetative propagation. Insects are the primary transmitters of phytoplasmas, but only after a three-week incubation period. After three weeks, the insect can transmit the phytoplasma for as long as the insect lives. This may have some important ramifications on controlling vectors of phytoplasma diseases.

Insects are frequently involved in the spread of fungal diseases as well. In many cases, the insect becomes coated with the pathogen as it moves among infected plants. For example, beetles that spread the oak wilt fungus (*Cerato-cystis fagacearum*) become coated with spores while feeding on an infected tree. Honeybees may become coated with the bacterial pathogen that causes fire blight when visiting infected trees. In cases where the disease pathogen is spread primarily by one vector, management methods focus on limiting the vector. Dutch elm disease (*Ophiostoma ulmi*), vectored by the native elm bark beetle (*Hylurgopinus rufipes*) and the smaller European elm bark beetle (*Scoly-tus multistriatus*), and bacterial wilt of cucumber (*Erwinia tracheiphila*), vectored by the striped cucumber beetle (*Acalymma vittatum*), are examples of such diseases. Plate 34 shows a bark beetle covered with fungal spores on a pine tree.

Humans as vectors of plant pathogens

By handling diseased and healthy plants in succession, humans can transmit virus diseases. To prevent the spread of tobacco mosaic virus (tobamovirus), a common disease of many greenhouse plants, greenhouse workers must avoid smoking in greenhouses and must frequently wash their hands. We also spread disease pathogens (particularly bacterial pathogens) on garden tools, in soil that we move around the garden, and on infected plants or plant parts that we bring to the garden or landscape. For example, Dutch elm disease was brought to the United States on imported timber. Citrus canker (*Xanthomonas campestris*) originated in Southeast Asia and has infected many areas of the United States. Its movement is now regulated by quarantines on propagation material and fruit.

Survival of the pathogen without the host

The final step in the disease cycle is the overwintering or oversummering of plant pathogens. In cold climates, this refers to survival of the pathogen during cold winter temperatures, often without a host. In warm climates, winter is not a factor, but the pathogen must be able to survive the heat and drought of summer, again often without a host.

The way a pathogen survives is very important to pathogen spread and therefore to disease management. Some survival forms include

- mycelium in infected plant tissues, for example, cankers on woody plant stems
- spores on bud scales, for example, anthracnose on tree hosts
- mycelium or spores on fallen leaves or fruit, for example, powdery mildew of many hosts and brown rot (*Monilinia fructicola*) of stone fruit
- sclerotia in soil or debris, for example, verticillium wilt
- bacteria on cankers and blighted twigs, for example, fire blight
- sclerotia on seed or other propagative organs, for example, hosta petiole blight (*Sclerotium rolfsii*), shown in plate 35.

Some pathogens, called *soil inhabitants*, can survive in the soil without any special needs. Those that can survive indefinitely as saprophytes include *Pythium*, *Fusarium*, and *Rhizoctonia*. All are common root rot pathogens of ornamental plants, fruits, and vegetables. Other pathogens, *soil transients*, usually require a plant host to survive but also may survive in the soil for short periods. Specialized spores of rust and downy mildews may survive as soil transients.

Most bacterial pathogens survive on or in host plants. In these cases, removal of infected plant material or debris is often very effective in reducing inoculum (the part of the disease-causing agent that can initiate infection). Crown gall, a common disease of woody ornamental plants such as rose and wintercreeper euonymus, is an exception. This bacterial pathogen, *Agrobacterium tumefaciens*, can survive in the soil without a host for many years and will re-infect susceptible plants that are planted in infested soil.

Some pathogens survive on hosts in the warmer climates and move northward by wind each year. Other pathogens live on an annual plant host during the growing season, move to a perennial plant host to overseason, and move back to the annual plant host the following growing season. *Coleosporium asterum*, which causes a rust disease, may overwinter on its pine host or in another spore stage on its alternate hosts, aster and goldenrod.

Viruses, viroids, phytoplasmas, fastidious bacteria, and protozoa survive only in association with a living plant host. The plant does not need to be actively growing, but it must be alive. Some viruses can overseason on bulbs such as tulips, which is why tulips exported from Holland to the United States are inspected before harvest. A few pathogens in this group can survive in their insect vectors. One such example is the fastidious bacterium that causes bacterial leaf scorch in oak, which is transmitted by certain leafhoppers. Once these leafhoppers are infected with the bacterium, they can transmit the pathogen for life. In addition, the bacterium that causes bacterial wilt of cucumber can survive in the striped cucumber beetle (*Acalymma vittatum*) vector.

Nematodes may overwinter as eggs in soil, or they may survive as eggs and nematodes in roots or plant debris. Pinewood nematode, the causal agent of pine wilt, overwinters in the wood, where it is protected against weather extremes. Foliar nematodes of hosta are sensitive to heat but are extremely cold hardy—they can overseason even in the northern United States.

Classification of disease cycles

Diseases may be monocyclic, polycyclic, or polyetic. Knowing the type of disease cycle will, in part, help to determine the appropriate management strategy to initiate.

Choosing effective disease control

Understanding how long-term pathogen survival occurs enables us to select effective disease-control options. Rotating annuals to another area of the garden might be effective for a disease such as rhizoctonia root rot, because the *Rhizoctonia* fungus can survive in the soil for many years without a host plant. Removing dead daylily leaves each fall on plants grown in the northern United States is helpful in controlling daylily rust because the fungus has not been shown to overwinter in the northern states, especially without host leaves.

MONOCYCLIC DISEASE. A disease that completes a single cycle per growing season or year is *monocyclic*. There is no secondary infection to intensify the disease. Reducing the initial severity of disease becomes very important in disease reduction and control. Soil-borne diseases such as root rots are monocyclic. Rotation is an effective measure to avoid disease infection in flowerbeds infested with *Fusarium* or *Rhizoctonia*.

Also monocyclic are the rust diseases that do not have a repeating stage. Cedar apple rust (*Gymnosporangium juniperi-virginianae*), shown in plate 36, is such a disease. All of the infection on crabapple results from the spores that come from the alternate host, Eastern redcedar (*Juniperus virginiana*). All of the infection on redcedar is the result of spores that came from the crabapple or apple host. Removal of the infected plant material may be an effective control measure.

POLYCYCLIC DISEASE. A disease that completes more than one disease cycle per growing season or year is *polycyclic*. The pathogen infects and reproduces as described above, and the newly formed inoculum causes further infection. Pathogens that cause polycyclic diseases are primarily air disseminated, and they develop and spread rapidly. Powdery mildew, shown on zinnia in plate 37, is a good example of a polycyclic disease. Because often the rate of spread is more important than the initial disease severity, sanitation measures (to reduce the amount of inoculum) are more effective for monocyclic diseases than for polycyclic diseases.

The control of polycyclic disease usually involves reducing the initial inoculum, and even more important, reducing secondary cycles. Pesticides may be the best choice for controlling polycyclic diseases. Apple scab is an example of this type of disease, and controls include:

- Resistant varieties of apple trees are planted where possible.
- Sanitation (removal of fallen leaves and other infected material) is performed to reduce initial inoculum.
- Trees are pruned to allow better air flow and discourage fungal growth.
- In some cases, pesticides are used to prevent secondary infection from occurring.

POLYETIC DISEASE. Some diseases of trees are *polyetic*, meaning that it takes more than one year to complete a disease cycle. The time required from infection to inoculum production, dissemination, and new infection on other host trees may be several years. The inoculum level is protected and preserved from year to year within the tree and can rapidly increase. Dutch elm disease and oak wilt, shown in plate 38, are prime examples of polyetic diseases that may be present in the landscape.

Plant pathogenesis

Pathogenicity is the ability of a pathogen to cause disease, and the degree of pathogenicity for a given pathogen is its *virulence*. A species that is avirulent does not cause a disease. For example, there are many pathogenic fungal anthracnose species on ornamental plants. The *Discula* species that is virulent (causes disease) on ash, shown in plate 39, is avirulent on dogwood.

Pathogenesis involves various mechanisms of attack by the pathogen as well as various responses by the plant. In his 1975 book *Plant Pathogenesis*, Harry Wheeler described pathogenesis as "a battle between a plant and a pathogen refereed by the environment." Although the steps of the disease cycle may seem to simplify the infection process, both the pathogen and the plant must overcome many barriers in the "battle" of pathogenesis. In addition, the process changes with time. To continue infection, the pathogen must

- find a susceptible host plant
- enter through the cellulose and cutin layers to the inside of cells
- break down the cell content to be absorbed
- neutralize the plant's defense mechanisms
- continue to break down cell walls

Mechanisms of attack

Pathogens use both mechanical forces and chemical compounds when they attack a plant. The available attack options vary with the pathogen, the host, and the environment. Mechanical forces include pressure exerted by some fungi, nematodes, and parasitic higher plants as they force their way into plant cells.

Fungal spores, which must adhere to the plant surface, often release enzymes such as cutinase and cellulase when they come in contact with water; and these enzymes help glue the spores to the surface. Then special hyphal structures called penetration pegs help the fungus to enter the plant. As these develop and grow from the spore, they push through the cuticle. If the host wall is too hard, then the pathogen may be unable to penetrate and infection will be stopped. However, enzymes that the fungus releases may counteract this barrier and help soften the tissue to allow entry.

Various chemicals that pathogens use may be categorized as enzymes, toxins, growth regulators, or polysaccharides. The importance of each differs with the disease. For example, enzymes are important in root rot infections and degradation of root tissue, whereas growth regulators play a role in the crown gall disease and overgrowth of cells. Although viruses and viroids cannot produce substances themselves, they can cause the plant cells to do so.

Although pathogens can use some cell components directly as food sources (for example, sugars), they must degrade others in order to absorb

---

How pathogens use enzymes

Various enzymes cause cell wall components to break down. Some break down the food substances in the cell so that fungi can absorb them. Enzymes also affect the components of the cell to interfere with metabolic functions. Most of the enzymes that pathogens produce and use to degrade structural components have names that match the material they degrade followed by the suffix -*ase*.

For example, *pectin* is a substance that cements cells together in a plant. The fungus that causes brown rot of flowering plum (*Monilinia fructicola*) produces pectinases or pectolytic enzymes that break down the pectin and result in soft rot. *Erwinia caratovora* (soft rot) and *Verticillium albo-atrum* (wilt) also produce pectinases to help in the infection process.

Cellulose is broken down by cellulases. Lignin, the structural component of wood, can be broken down by ligninases produced by only a few fungi such as the white rot fungi. The fungus that causes Dutch elm disease (*Ophiostoma ulmi*) synthesizes pectolytic and cellulolytic enzymes that affect cell walls and pit membranes in the xylem vessels of the elm.

them. Pathogen enzymes help to degrade some of these cell components: Proteases degrade cell proteins; amylases and lipids degrade starches by lipolytic enzymes. Various pathogens produce these pathogen enzymes. For example, the bacterial pathogen that causes ring rot of potato, *Clavibacter michiganensis,* is known to produce proteinases that cause degradation of cell proteins in potatoes and other host plants.

Pathogens also may use growth regulators during the infection process, causing plant cells to grow abnormally. Symptoms may include galls, epinasty (downward curvature of plant parts such as leaves), and witches' brooms. Both bacteria and fungi may produce growth regulators such as auxins, gibberellins, cytokinins, and ethylene. Auxin is involved in gall formation by plants infected with *Agrobacterium tumefaciens,* the causal agent of crown gall of many ornamentals. Some *Fusarium* species produce ethylene, which causes epinasty symptoms.

Pathogens also may produce toxins. Usually the toxin interferes in some way with cell permeability and cell functions. *Pseudomonas syringae* produces psyringomycin, which injures the tender new growth of some woody ornamentals in the spring. Amylovorin is a pathotoxin produced as a result of an interaction between the plant and a bacterial pathogen, *Erwinia amylovora,* which causes fire blight. This toxin causes stem cankers, wilting of shoots, and blackening of infected plant parts.

Polysaccharides are involved primarily with vascular diseases. These chemicals, which the pathogen produces, cause passive interference to water translocation. Some are also toxic.

Plant responses to pathogens

Plants do possess some defense mechanisms, both structural and biochemical, to use in response to a pathogen attack. They also possess some normal structural and chemical defenses whether or not a pathogen attacks. In some cases, the plant's defensive reaction may prevent infection and result in plant resistance to the pathogen. In other cases, defenses merely slow the spread of the pathogen. Serious diseases occur when the plant responses cannot stop the pathogen.

Structural defenses

Plants have anatomic features that may slow or even stop infection. Some plants have a thick waxy coating or thick cuticle that poses a physical barrier to bacterial and fungal invasion. There may be stomata and lenticels with small openings that help prevent intrusion by the pathogen. Often a hairy leaf serves as a protective mechanism. The size of xylem vessels also may be a factor, because the shorter, smaller diameter vessels are easier for the tree to plug. Because quick plugging of the xylem is a resistance mechanism against the Dutch elm disease fungus, this anatomic quality is an important defense against disease.

Biochemical defenses

Plants defend themselves with biochemical mechanisms that are not expressed when the plants are healthy but are induced by a pathogen. Once a pathogen enters the plant, there are all sorts of defense reactions by the plant:

- formation of intracellular protuberances
- formation of cork layers
- formation of abscission layers to cause leaf drop
- overgrowth of parenchyma into the xylem (tyloses)
- production of gums

Chapter 5, which addresses cultural pest management, includes a discussion of these mechanisms.

Induced biochemical defenses against the pathogen are very complex. In infected plants, the permeability of cells may be disrupted, causing infected cells to leak large quantities of electrolytes and lose the ability to accumulate minerals. This phenomenon is seen with bacterial diseases that exhibit water-soaked areas around the infection site, such as bacterial blotch of watermelon (*Acidovorax avenae* subsp. *citrulli*), shown in plate 40. The water relations in a plant may be disrupted in response to the vascular wilt diseases. Wilting results from the plant's inability to absorb water, inability to transport water, and dysfunction of stomata. All of these functions are interrelated and necessary for plant growth and development.

For example, there may be an accumulation of starches and other materials around infection sites because the plant cannot translocate them where needed. Often this appears as small islands of green tissue on otherwise yellowed leaves or stems. The green areas are rich in starches and other accumulated products. Other biochemical defenses induced by the presence of the pathogen are the reinforcement of plant cell walls with strengthening molecules and the production of antimicrobial substances.

Of all of the pathogens that land on plants in the landscape, only a small percentage cause disease. To understand how and why disease occurs, it helps to find out about the various host pathogen interactions for the disease identified. This information is invaluable in choosing control options that will most effectively manage the disease.

Chapter 3

Needs of Insects, Mites, and Mollusks

The management of insects, mites, mollusks, and other pests in home landscapes and gardens involves reducing the ability of these pests to survive, thrive, and reproduce. Logic tells us that anything that increases stress to the pest will decrease its ability to damage plants. This chapter addresses the physiological needs of insects and their relatives, as well as their life cycles, feeding habits, and other activities.

All organisms, including insects, need food, water, and shelter. Although insects obtain food from garden and landscape plants, the plants do not simply allow insects to feed upon them; rather, they defend themselves both physically and physiologically. They defend themselves physically with thick leaf surfaces, rinds and shells on fruits and nuts, bark on trunks, leaf hairs, and spines. They defend themselves physiologically by using a wide array of compounds that affect insects' ability to function.

Characteristics of insects

Insects have several defining characteristics. Although other animals may have one or two of these characteristics, insects have many of them. Insects are segmented animals with segmented legs, mouthparts, and other appendages.

HEAD, THORAX, AND ABDOMEN. The body segments of insects are combined physically and functionally into three regions: head, thorax, and abdomen.

Casual insect groupings

Appendix C lists the scientific names for many insects mentioned throughout this book. However, many of the common insect names most familiar to us all, such as butterfly, actually represent informal groups of insects with similar characteristics. For these insect groups, it would be impossible to give a scientific name, because multiple species in multiple genera are involved. Examples include aphids, bees, butterflies, cockroaches, damselflies, dragonflies, earwigs, flies, grasshoppers, grubs, lacewings, leafhoppers, mayflies, mealybugs, plant bugs, praying mantids, psyllids, scales, silverfish, snails, springtails, stink bugs, stoneflies, walkingsticks, wasps, weevils, and whiteflies.

The head is involved with sensory functions and feeding. It has one pair of antennae, chewing or sucking mouthparts, compound eyes made up of many simple eyes, plus possibly one to three simple eyes on the top of the head. The head also contains the brain.

The thorax is the region behind the head and is primarily associated with locomotion, with three pairs of legs attached to it. Adults typically have two pairs of wings on the thorax, but flies and some other insects have one pair of wings and many insects are wingless as adults. Muscles that drive the legs and wings take up most of the space inside the thorax.

The abdomen, the posterior region of the body, carries out most of the physiological functions. Typically, the only external structures are reproductive. Inside the abdomen is the heart, most of the digestive system, excretion system, reproductive organs, and most of the respiratory system.

LEGS AND PROLEGS. Although insects typically have three pairs of legs as adults, insect larvae may have more or fewer. Caterpillars typically have three pairs of true legs, but they also have five pairs of fleshy, unsegmented legs called *prolegs*. Plate 41 shows a variable oakleaf caterpillar (*Lochmaeus manteo*), which has five pairs of prolegs. Each proleg has hooks on the end that helps the caterpillar hang onto plants. Some caterpillars, loopers and cankerworms, have only two or three pairs of prolegs toward the end of the abdomen.

Sawfly larvae have six to nine pairs of prolegs without hooks on the end. The introduced pine sawfly larva (*Diprion similis*) in plate 42, for example, has eight pairs. This distinction is important because the bacterial insecticide *Bacillus thuringiensis kurstaki* (Btk) is effective against caterpillars, the larval stage of butterflies and moths. It is not effective against sawfly larvae, which are closely related to wasps. Although the general appearance of caterpillars and sawfly larvae is similar, the number of prolegs can distinguish them.

Several kinds of insect larvae are legless, but the adults will have three pairs of legs. The saddleback caterpillar (*Sibine stimulea*) and its relatives are legless, as are borer larvae of moths and beetles. Other insects that are legless as larvae include flies, ants, bees, wasps, and fleas.

EGGS. Although the eggs of many insects are oval and translucent white, there are exceptions:

- The eggs of the ladybird beetle are yellow and pointed.
- The eggs of some assassin bugs are blackish, tall, and slender.
- The eggs of the squash bug (*Anasa tristis*) and of the squash vine borer (*Melittia cucurbitae*) are round and red.
- The eggs of some pine aphid species are black.

Butterflies, aphids, flies, bees, wasps, and dragonflies tend to lay eggs individually, making them difficult to see. Many moths, assassin bugs, and stink bugs lay their eggs in clusters on the undersides of leaves. Plate 43 shows such an egg mass from a yellownecked caterpillar (*Datana ministra*). Grasshoppers and praying mantids lay cases, each containing 30 to 100 eggs or more. Grasshoppers, field crickets, and earwigs lay their eggs in clusters underground, where garden tillage exposes them to drying out and predators. Tree crickets, plant bugs, cicadas, leafhoppers, sawflies, and thrips lay their egg clusters in plant tissue. Plate 44 shows damage from egg clusters of the periodical cicada (*Magicicada septendecim*).

Insect exoskeleton

Instead of having a skeleton on the inside of the body, as do humans and other vertebrates, insects have a skeleton outside the body, called an *exoskeleton*. The exoskeleton is *chitinous*, meaning that it is flexible like human fingernails. Where a very rigid structure is needed, the inside of the exoskeleton is

The mighty muscles of insects

Because an insect's muscles are inside the exoskeleton, it is easy for muscle to attach close to the end of each leg segment. This enables the muscles to create much greater force without increasing in size. In part, this is why a flea can jump many times its own height, a wasp can fly with many times its own weight, and an ant can carry or drag many times its own weight.

strengthened with ridges similar to the girders of a building. Advantages to having a hard-shelled exoskeleton are that it

- enables insects to burrow through soil, wood, and other materials without being crushed
- protects them from some predators that do not have jaws strong enough to crush them
- reduces water loss
- allows the muscles to create much greater force without increasing in size

A major disadvantage of an exoskeleton is its weight. For a small animal, the weight is not a major concern, but as an animal grows, muscle mass must increase considerably to handle the extra weight. This relates to what is perhaps the most serious disadvantage of an exoskeleton: It cannot grow. Once an insect grows to fill the exoskeleton, it must be *molted* (shed) and replaced. As the insect grows, it must molt and produce a new exoskeleton several times.

The molting process

As the insect prepares to molt, it releases enzymes on the inside of the old exoskeleton to dissolve it partially, making the components available for formation of a new exoskeleton. As this is occurring, muscle attachment sites and other important attachments to the old exoskeleton are loosened and become less functional. This reduces the insect's ability to move away from danger or toward food.

During molting, the outer portion of the exoskeleton that has not been dissolved splits, typically along the back, and the insect pulls itself out of its old skeleton. Plate 45 shows an adult annual cicada (*Tibicen*) molting from the nymph. It is common for a leg or another body part to stick in the old exoskeleton. This makes the insect very vulnerable to predation, or leaves the insect unable to move around and feed, causing it to die of starvation.

After a successful molt, the insect's new skeleton is still flexible. The insect inhales air to increase the size of the exoskeleton so that it has some room to grow before it must molt again. While it is soft, the exoskeleton is typically whitish, which makes the insect obvious to predators. Furthermore, the insect's muscles are less effective soon after molting because the attachment points on the exoskeleton are still soft. The insect is very vulnerable to predators while its exoskeleton is still soft and easily crushed.

Because insects are so vulnerable to predators during molting and soon after, they commonly stop feeding and hide before molting. They typically molt during the night so that their exoskeleton is tanned and hardened (allowing them to be fully mobile) soon after daybreak.

Caterpillars and other insect pests commonly cease to feed for two to three days while they molt. Because all of the same species of caterpillar or other insect on a plant may have hatched from the same egg cluster, progressive insect damage may seem to stop for two or three days during this molting time, but typically damage will increase with greater speed because older, larger insects generally eat more than younger, smaller stage insects. Caterpillars eat 94 to 98 percent of the food that they will consume during the last two larval stages between larval molts, or *instars*. Immature insects grow exponentially, often doubling their weight during each instar. Full-grown larvae often weigh several thousand times more than they do at hatching time.

Metamorphosis

When implementing IPM of insects, it is important to understand their life cycles, because insects are more susceptible to control during certain life stages than they are in other stages. It also is important to know when in their life cycle they cause damage to landscape or garden plants, so that they can be controlled beforehand.

Insects have two main types of life cycles, also called development or metamorphosis. *Metamorphosis* refers to a change in structure or function of an insect as it develops and moves through its life cycle. The two main classifications are simple metamorphosis and complete metamorphosis. Intermediate metamorphosis occurs in a few types of insects that have characteristics of both simple and complete metamorphosis.

Simple metamorphosis

Simple metamorphosis insects have three life-cycle stages: egg, nymph, and adult. Adult insects mate, and then the female lays eggs that hatch into nymphs. These nymphs grow up and molt into adults. Examples of insects that undergo simple metamorphosis include springtails, silverfish, mayflies, dragonflies, stoneflies, grasshoppers, praying mantids, walkingsticks, plant bugs, stink bugs, squash bugs, chinch bugs (*Blissus leucopterus leucopterus*), cicadas, leafhoppers, aphids, and earwigs.

Nymphs resemble adults except that they are smaller, have no wings, and cannot reproduce. Furthermore, their body parts are in slightly different proportion than they will be as adults. In winged insects, the wings develop on the outside of the body as wing buds or wing pads that get larger and more obvious as the insect develops. Both nymph and adult boxelder bugs (*Boisea trivittata*) are shown in plate 46. Grasshopper nymphs and praying mantis nymphs have legs that are proportionally longer and a head proportionally

Types of simple metamorphosis

Some entomologists consider mayflies, dragonflies, and stoneflies to be *hemimetabolous*. In these insects, the nymphs are commonly called naiads, are aquatic with gills, and look quite different from the adults. The rest of the insects with simple metamorphosis are called *paurometabolous*. In these insects, the nymphs and adults live in the same habitat and eat similar food, and the adults have wings. Most of them are terrestrial.

Finally, some entomologists consider springtails, silverfish, and related insects to be *ametabolous*, meaning that they have no metamorphosis. The only obvious difference in these insects between nymphs and adults is size. The adults are wingless.

larger than in adults of their species. Newly hatched aphids have legs almost as long as the adults, but their bodies are much smaller.

As a nymph develops and grows, it sheds its exoskeleton in a process called *molting*. A nymph commonly goes through five molts, but this too varies among species. Remember, *instars* are the stages between the nymphal molts. Thus, an egg hatches into a first instar nymph, grows and molts into the second instar, then third instar, fourth instar, fifth instar, and eventually adult.

Adult insects neither grow larger nor molt. They can reproduce, and females have structures for egg laying. Wings are present only in the adult stage.

Nymphs and adults typically feed on the same food and in the same way. Nymphal and adult grasshoppers, katydids, and walkingsticks bite off pieces of leaves, and nymphal and adult praying mantids bite off pieces of their prey. Both the nymphs and adults of aphids, leafhoppers, cicadas, some stink bugs, chinch bugs, and plant bugs suck plant juices. Nymphs and adults of ambush bugs, assassin bugs, and some stink bugs suck insect juices.

CONTROLLING INSECT PESTS UNDERGOING SIMPLE METAMORPHOSIS. Typically with these pests, it is necessary to control them in one location only. For example, grasshoppers are controlled in flowerbeds with only one concentrated effort, because both the nymphs and the adults are present on the same plants at the same time and both are controlled with the same methods. Likewise, nymphal and adult aphids are usually present on the same plant at the same time—so again, one control action usually controls both life stages.

Complete metamorphosis

Although the immature stage or nymph of an insect with simple metamorphosis is similar in appearance, habits, and food to the adult, the immature stage or larva of an insect with complete metamorphosis is generally completely different from the adult in those attributes. Adults lay eggs that hatch into larvae. The larvae go through three instars or more, molting to the next stage, and they live in a different habitat than do adults. Fully grown larvae molt into pupae from which the adults emerge. Plate 47 shows cottonwood leaf beetle (*Chrysomela scripta*) eggs and pupae. Insects with complete metamorphosis include butterflies, moths, beetles, lacewings, flies, sawflies, ants, bees, and wasps.

Mouthparts and feeding habits of larvae versus adults

Because the food of larvae is commonly different from that of adults of the same species, the mouthparts are frequently different as well.

- Caterpillars have chewing mouthparts that bite off chunks of leaves or wood for food, whereas adult butterflies and moths have sucking mouthparts in the form of an elongated tube that siphons flower nectar and other nutritious fluids.
- Bee larvae have chewing mouthparts for feeding on pollen and nectar that the adults bring to them, whereas adult bees have sucking mouthparts for imbibing flower nectar.
- Lacewing and ground beetle larvae have long mouthparts that suck juices out of their prey. The adults have chewing mouthparts that they use to devour their prey.
- House fly (*Musca domestica*), blow fly (*Phormia*), flesh fly (*Sarcophaga*), and related fly larvae have simple mouth hooks to rake in manure and rotting flesh. The adults have sucking mouthparts—either a sponge-like structure for absorbing liquid food, or a piercing structure for obtaining blood.

Some larvae have mouthparts that are similar to those of adults. Sawflies, wasps, ants, and most beetles have chewing mouthparts both as larvae and as adults. However, the food source of the immature and the adult are frequently different, resulting in their living in different habitats.

CONTROLLING INSECT PESTS UNDERGOING COMPLETE METAMORPHOSIS. Because larvae typically live in different habitats and feed on different food sources than do adults, management of these insect pests is more difficult. Management of insects that undergo complete metamorphosis requires frequent scouting and knowledge of the habits of both the larva and the adult. The larvae of imported cabbageworm (*Pieris rapae*) may be controlled on broccoli and cabbage in the garden, but the adults—white butterflies—are feeding elsewhere on flower nectar and will return to the broccoli and cabbage to lay eggs.

The pupa stage is a nonfeeding stage in which the larva changes into the adult. Pupae are commonly reddish-brown. The adult legs, antennae, mouth-parts, and wings are visible on many beetle, wasp, ant, bee, and moth pupae. Plate 48 shows a cutworm pupa. Outlines of the adult moth's wings and abdominal segments are visible.

Another characteristic of insects that undergo complete metamorphosis is that wing development does not appear externally until the pupal stage. Pupae typically are very limited in movement, being restricted to moving the abdomen or rolling about if disturbed. Many caterpillars, sawfly larvae, and other insects pupate within a silk covering called a *cocoon*. A cocoon of a cecropia moth (*Hyalophora cecropia*) is shown in plate 49.

Intermediate metamorphosis

Although thrips, whiteflies, mealybugs, and scales are considered to have in-complete metamorphosis, their development closely parallels complete meta-morphosis. Whiteflies, mealybugs, and scales hatch from the egg into an active stage, already able to crawl around on the plant. First instar mealybugs and scales are called crawlers, and this is the only stage at which they are able to disperse. Subsequent immature stages of whiteflies, mealybugs, and scales are sessile on (attached to) the plant. Whiteflies, in all immature stages except the last one, are called larvae. Whiteflies, male mealybugs, and scales in their last immature stage, which is inactive, are called pupae.

The first two immature stages of thrips are usually called larvae or nymphs, and some species have internal wing development. The next two stages are called prepupae and pupae. In these stages, thrips are relatively in-active, and their wings develop externally. Adults then emerge from the pupae.

The development of mites and other insect relatives

Mites undergo incomplete metamorphosis but hatch from eggs into six-legged larvae. When the larva molts, it emerges as an eight-legged nymph, which molts into an eight-legged adult. After adults mate, the female lays eggs. Spiders, which are close relatives of mites, hatch as eight-legged imma-tures that have habits similar to their eight-legged adult counterparts.

Mites feed on liquids of various types. The most familiar plant-feeding mites are spider mites, such as twospotted spider mite (*Tetranychus urticae*), and spruce spider mite (*Oligonychus ununguis*). They are roughly spherical and very tiny, being barely visible on host leaves without magnification. They spin very fine silk over the leaves and between the leaves and stem. This silk is finer than spider silk and is easily seen in the early morning when there is still dew on the webbing, illuminated by the low-angled light from the morning sun. The silk is so fine that it is easily blown away or destroyed by rain.

Eriophyid mites, much smaller than spider mites, are visible only with a hand lens or microscope. They are elongate, cigar-shaped animals that are broad anteriorly and tapered posteriorly. They have only four legs at the anterior end of the body. Their feeding commonly results in distorted leaves, usually at the tip of the branch, and blasted buds. Other species' feeding results in rust-like leaf symptoms or gall formation.

Predatory mites feed primarily on other mites. They are usually fast moving but otherwise similar in general appearance to spider mites. Commonly, they are numerous enough that they keep spider mites from becoming pest problems. Some predatory mites have become specialized as parasites on birds (such as the northern fowl mite, *Ornithonyssus sylviarum*) and mammals (such as the itch mite, *Sarcoptes scabiei*). Ticks, such as the American dog tick (*Dermacentor variabilis*), are very large parasitic mites that commonly attack birds, mammals, and other vertebrates. They are flattened to avoid being brushed off by their host.

Many mite species are scavengers, feeding on dead materials. They are common in mulches, accumulations of fallen leaves, and soil. Although many are small and whitish, the oribatid mites are spherical mites that are typically brown or black. Oribatid mites are about 0.03 inch in diameter, making them easy to see crawling in the soil.

Centipedes and millipedes are insect relatives that hatch with fewer legs than they have as adults. They pass through many molts, adding legs along the way. Although crayfish start out small but fully formed, many other crustaceans undergo various larval stages in which they appear quite different from adults.

Chewing insects and their damage

There are two major types of insect mouthparts, chewing and sucking. Chewing mouthparts, which are the most common, are made up of toothed mandibles (jaws) that can bite off chunks of food. Insects incorporate metallic elements into the mandibles to make them harder and more efficient in chewing food. Associated mouthparts manipulate the food—bringing it into the mouth and moving it around inside the mouth—so that the mandibles can chew it.

Examples of insects with chewing mouthparts include

- nymphs and adults of dragonflies, grasshoppers, crickets, praying mantids, walkingsticks, and earwigs
- caterpillars
- larvae and adults of most beetles
- bee larvae
- larvae and adults of sawflies, wasps, and ants

WINDOW-FEEDING. The larvae of leaf beetles such as elm leaf beetle (Pyrrhalta luteola), willow leaf beetle, and cottonwood leaf beetle, as well as many young caterpillars, eat through the lower epidermis (leaf surface) and consume the mesophyll (interior of the leaf), leaving the upper epidermis intact. Because the mesophyll contains most of the green chlorophyll and the upper epidermis is light in color to clear, the damaged part of the leaf at first appears as a whitish to clear area. This is called window-feeding. Eventually the exposed epidermis tissues dry and turn brown. Plate 50 shows an elm leaf beetle larva on a leaf, and the associated window-feeding damage.

SKELETONIZATION. When insects eat all the way through the leaf, the result is skeletonization. Small veins may be left uneaten, but usually all but the major veins are consumed. Older caterpillars, most sawfly larvae, Colorado potato beetle (*Leptinotarsa decemlineata*) larvae and adults, and adult leaf beetles begin feeding at the leaf margin and remove large areas of the leaf, leaving only the major veins intact. Japanese beetle (*Popillia japonica*), hollyhock weevil (*Apion longirostre*), flea beetle, roseslug (*Endelomyia aethiops*), and some other insects commonly feed on the leaf surface, away from the edge. As a result, their damage to leaves appears lacelike with many of the small veins intact, as shown with Japanese beetle adults in plate 51.

DEFOLIATION. Sometimes, as shown in plate 52, the entire leaf is consumed or perhaps only the main leaf vein and stubs of lesser veins remain. This damage is characteristic of mature caterpillars and large adult beetles. Often, severe skeletonization or even window-feeding causes the remaining portion of the leaf to fall off, resulting in defoliation.

TUNNELING AND BORING. Chewing mouthparts also allow an insect to tunnel into plant material, consuming it as it tunnels. These insect borers damage various plant parts. Bronze birch borer (*Agrilus anxius*), flatheaded appletree borer (*Chrysobothris femorata*), and other flatheaded borers tunnel into the cambium (the layer between the xylem and the phloem) and wood of trees and shrubs. Because these larvae are broad and oval, they create oval tunnels in the wood, as shown with the honeylocust borer (*Agrilus difficilis*) in plate 53. The larvae pupate within the wood, and the adults must bore their way out. These adults are flattened on their underside, but their upper side is rounded. As a result, they create D-shaped emergence holes.

Caterpillar wood borers such as Zimmerman pine moth (*Dioryctria zimmermani*), squash vine borer, ash/lilac borer (*Podosesia syringae*), viburnum borer, peachtree borer (*Synanthedon exitiosa*), and dogwood borer (*S. scitula*) are circular in cross section as larvae. Cottonwood borer (*Plectrodera scalator*), redheaded ash borer (*Neoclytus acuminatus*), Asian longhorned beetle (*Anoplophora glabripennis*), locust borer (*Megacyllene robiniae*), painted hickory borer (*M. caryae*), and other roundheaded borers are circular in cross section both as adults and as larvae. These insects create circular tunnels in the wood and circular emergence holes.

Borers also are found in other plant parts:

- The larvae of young billbugs (*Sphenophorus*) tunnel in the stems and rhizomes of turfgrasses.
- The larvae of codling moths (*Cydia pomonella*), oriental fruit moths (*Grapholita molesta*), and plum curculios (*Conotrachelus nenuphar*) tunnel through the fruit of apples, peaches, plums, and other trees, depending on their host preference.
- The larvae of Nantucket pine tip moths (*Rhyacionia frustrana*), European pine shoot moths (*R. buoliana*), and Zimmerman pine moths tunnel into the shoots growing at the end of stems.
- The larvae of Corn rootworms (*Diabrotica*), the older larvae of

Specialized borers

Leafminers are very specialized borers. These larvae of flies, wasps, moths, beetles, and caterpillars have adapted to live on the mesophyll (internal tissues of the leaf) between the epidermises (upper and lower leaf surfaces). Typically, the adult female inserts her egg into the leaf, but in some species, the female lays her egg on the leaf surface. In both cases, the hatched larva tunnels through the mesophyll, creating a light-colored leaf area. This area eventually dries and turns brown. The tunnels these leafminers create varies. For example,

- Columbine leafminers (*Phytomyza*) and leafminers in honeysuckle (*Swezeyula lonicerae*) create serpentine mines that are narrow, winding tunnels.
- Oak leafminer (*Cameraria*), birch leafminer (*Fenusa pusilla*), and European alder leafminer (*F. dohrnii*) create blotch mines that are large roundish or angulate areas between major leaf veins.
- Holly leafminer (*Phytomyza ilicis*) and beet leafminer (*Pegomya betae*) create serpentine mines as young larvae and blotch mines as older larvae.

Plate 54 shows the feeding damage of the holly leafminer (both younger and older larval mines).

billbugs, and white grubs tunnel in underground plant parts, such as roots and tubers.

GALLMAKING. Gallmakers typically lay eggs on or in the young, undifferentiated plant tissue that grows at the tips of stems and roots, in buds, and in developing leaves. In response to the mechanical damage or chemical substances that the gallmaker produces, the young plant tissue grows around and encloses the insect in a tumor-like formation. The gallmaker lives within the gall and feeds on its tissue. The ash midrib gall in plate 55 has been split open to show its interior and the inhabitant insect (*Contarinia canadensis*) larva.

The gallmaker has a reliable food source in a moist environment, protected from most predators. Few attacked plants seem to be seriously harmed, because plants with galls grow just as well as those without galls. Various flies, wasps, psyllids (sucking insects also known as jumping plant lice), and mites have adapted to life as gallmakers. It is possible to identify the species of gall-maker by the shape, size, and other characteristics of the gall that the host plant forms. Gallmaking wasps and oaks have a particularly strong relationship: Hundreds of wasp species cause gall formation in numerous species of oak.

Sucking insects and their damage

The mouthparts of sucking insects are shaped like elongated tubes for ingesting liquid food. Typically, these insects feed on fluids of either living plants or living animals. They damage plants by removing plant fluids from cells, the xylem, or the phloem. Examples of sucking insects are aphids, scales, mealybugs, leafhoppers, cicadas, stink bugs, plant bugs, assassin bugs, thrips, lacewing larvae, and adult bees and flies. Some insect relatives—mites, spiders, and centipedes—also have sucking mouthparts.

LEAF FEEDING. When feeding, plant bugs and spider mites pierce the epidermis into the mesophyll and suck out the cell contents. This removal of green chlorophyll-containing tissue causes that area of the leaf to appear whitish. Eventually, the cells dry and turn brown. Heavy leaf feeding causes many white or brown dots called *stippling*, as shown in plate 56. From a distance, white stippling damage on green leaves causes the leaves to appear light green or even white, resembling frost in heavy infestations; and brown stippling damage causes leaves to appear bronze.

If enough sap and other liquids are removed, piercing-sucking leaf feeding causes the leaf to turn yellowish, curl, and sometimes fall off. Occasionally, it causes large areas of the leaf to turn brown. Feeding on expanding leaves causes the leaves to become distorted and twisted lengthwise or curled horizontally, as shown in plate 57. Thrips and aphids commonly inflict this type of damage on leaves at the tips of tree branches. Aphids feeding on young stems can cause them to twist and curl as well. Feeding by scales and mealybugs creates yellow spots on stems and leaves.

FLOWER PETAL FEEDING. The flower thrips (*Frankliniella tritici*), western flower thrips (*F. occidentalis*), tarnished plant bug, and some aphid species feed on

Piercing-sucking insects as vectors

Viruses and phytoplasmas can cause damage to plants that is similar to the types of damage described here. Because piercing-sucking insects are common vectors of viruses and phytoplasmas, it can be difficult to differentiate between injury by plant pathogens and the direct mechanical and feeding injury by insects. Research continues to reveal injury previously diagnosed as insect feeding to be partially or totally caused by plant pathogens transmitted by the attacking insect. In many cases, therefore, injury caused by the pathogen is more important than the insect's feeding damage.

flower petals, causing whitish streaks or blotches that eventually turn brown. Plate 58 shows white streaking on chrysanthemum flowers. Areas of white streaking on white and yellow flowers may not become noticeable until the areas turn brown.

FRUIT FEEDING. Stink bugs, aphids, and tarnished plant bugs (*Lygus lineolaris*) feed on young fruit, causing catfacing (sunken areas that coalesce into lines) and dimples on apples. When the cells of young fruit are injured, they do not divide and expand as the rest of the fruit grows. These areas appear to be sunken as the fruit grows larger, because the damaged cells stay small.

BARK-FEEDING. Insects that feed through the bark of stems, twigs, and trunks include several scales, the pine bark adelgid (*Pineus strobi*), spittlebugs, treehoppers, and leafhoppers. Feeding causes branches to die back, and severe infestations can kill the plant.

Nutrient needs of insects

The nutrient needs of insects are similar to those of other animals, but there are some exceptions. Only magnesium is as plentiful in plants as it is in insects. To obtain other substances, insects must consume large amounts of plant tissue to achieve the nutrients and energy they need. Unlike many other animals, insects cannot manufacture sterols. Insects obtain amino acids, carbohydrates, lipids, fatty acids, sterols, vitamins, and trace elements from their food. Depending on the insect, the proportions of these needs vary. For example, the larvae of corn earworms (*Helicoverpa zea*) develop quickly and need high protein levels, but are relatively inactive insects. They grow best on a diet that has almost four times as much protein as carbohydrate. Conversely, cockroach nymphs are very active. Because they require high levels of carbohydrates but develop slowly, they do better on a diet that has over five times as much carbohydrate as protein.

Nitrogen

Caloric value is a measure of energy, and the caloric value of plants is only slightly less than that of insects. Mammals tend to grow slowly but use more energy; therefore, the caloric value of plants is more critical for them. Insects grow faster; therefore, their need for nitrogen is higher than their need for calories.

Plants tend to lack nitrogen in a form that insects can use. The dry weight of insects and other animals typically ranges from 8 to 14 percent nitrogen, but plants overall contain only 2 to 4 percent nitrogen. Even more important for sap-feeding insects is that phloem sap contains only 0.5 percent nitrogen or less, and xylem fluid contains 0.1 percent nitrogen or less. Seed and leaves typically contain from 1 to 5 percent nitrogen or more.

Nitrogen is very important for insect growth and reproduction, but to be useful to insects, it must be combined with other chemicals. Sometimes plants have nitrogen-containing chemicals such as alkaloids and tannins that actually reduce insect digestion.

Water

Although water is not a nutrient, it is vital for life functions. Because the leaves of plants typically contain 45 to 95 percent water, insects in gardens and landscapes have an abundant source. It has been shown that caterpillars developed 40 percent more slowly on leaves containing less water though not wilted. Of the caterpillar species tested, the tree-feeders tended to respond better to extra water than those that fed on low-growing plants.

Caterpillars lose water faster than other insects do. By contrast, grasshoppers show less change in development as the water content of their host plant

The nitrogen-pest connection

In general, plants that contain high nitrogen levels are more useful to insects than plants with lesser amounts. Therefore, fertilizing plants with nitrogen commonly results in the faster growth and reproduction of some insects, resulting in greater damage to plants. However, many insects grow less rapidly with increased nitrogen. The response of insect pests to nitrogen levels in plants depends on the insect involved. Western spruce budworm (*Choristoneura occidentalis*) develops better at lower nitrogen levels. Aphids, whiteflies, soft scales, and spider mites grow faster and reproduce more on higher nitrogen food.

decreases. In fact, desert grasshoppers tend to be more attracted to water-stressed plants than to normal plants. It may be that drought stress causes plants to reduce the amount of chemicals that deter feeding and to increase the levels of nutrients that insects need. Drought and other stresses to plants result in increased levels of soluble sugars and nitrogen in leaves, inner bark, and sapwood.

Water and leaf nitrogen levels are associated in plants, particularly in higher amounts of nitrogen-containing protein and amino acids when water is plentiful. Young leaves tend to have higher levels of water and protein than mature or senescing leaves. In general, tree leaves normally contain less water and nitrogen than leaves of lower-growing plants. Nutritional levels in plants tend to decrease later in the summer.

Plant substances of little use to insects

Plants contain a variety of substances that either are of little or no use to insects, or actually reduce the ability of insects to feed and develop. For example, insects cannot digest cellulose and lignin, which plants rely on heavily for structural support. Wood-boring beetles and the other few insects that use wood and other cellulose for food actually rely on microorganisms to digest the cellulose. Insects digest the breakdown products, the microorganisms, or both, but they do not digest the intact cellulose.

Feeding habits

Insects consuming a nutritionally poor food source will eat more of it—a factor called *compensatory feeding*. In fact, an insect will eat up to seven times as much to compensate for a poor quality food source. The insect has both external and internal sensors which can determine that more food or higher quality food needs to be eaten.

There are tradeoffs for an insect faced with nutritionally poor food, however. As the insect eats more food, the food stays in the insect's digestive tract for a shorter time, resulting in decreased absorption of the available nutrients. Because the relative amounts of protein and carbohydrate vary in the foods eaten, consuming more food to obtain enough protein may result in the consumption of too much carbohydrate or vice versa. Increased food intake may also expose the insect to higher levels of allelochemicals (chemicals plants produce that deter insect feeding or are poisonous to insects) and perhaps overload mechanisms that cope with these chemicals. Through food selection, an insect may opt to eat large amounts of a less nutritious food that is also low in allelochemicals rather than a nutritious food that is high in allelochemicals.

Increased food consumption tends to expose an insect to predation. While feeding, caterpillars are 100 times more likely to be eaten by a predator. When not feeding, caterpillars tend to remain hidden on the undersides of leaves, along a branch, or in other concealed locations. Even a motionless insect in full view is much less obvious to a predator than an insect that is moving while feeding.

Allelochemicals

As we just mentioned, plants produce *allelochemicals*, which are chemicals that deter insects from feeding or are harmful to them. Generally, insects must avoid or detoxify these chemicals, and this requires an additional expenditure of energy. Research has shown that herbivorous insects actually grow and develop better on an artificial diet lacking allelochemicals than they do feeding on their host plants. (For example, the larvae of black cutworms, *Agrotis ipsilon*, grow twelve times faster on an artificial diet than they do on corn leaves.) As allelochemicals are added to the artificial diet, their effects on the insect become evident. In fact, insects that are predatory and parasitoid (par-

Tannins

Common in the leaves of oaks and other trees, tannins apparently bind to leaf proteins or digestive enzymes in the insect gut, inhibiting digestion. These allelochemicals also have been shown to inhibit insect feeding, induce lesions in the gut, and produce toxic effects. However some insects have adapted to them. One tree grasshopper species grows 15 percent faster when tannic acid is added to its artificial diet.

asitic) obtain food that is better balanced for their needs than do insects that are herbivorous (feed on plants).

Allelochemicals impact insects in three different ways:

- They can reduce food intake by inhibiting feeding.
- Once eaten, they can adversely affect the use of the food.
- They can function as a poison by interfering with the physiological functions of the insect.

Commonly, all three mechanisms are involved.

The activity of allelochemicals is most noticeable on *nonadapted insects*—insects that are unable to feed or grow at all on a plant because of allelochemicals. However, allelochemicals apparently inhibit even *adapted insects*—insects that are able to grow and reproduce on plants that contain them.

Plants typically possess not only one allelochemical, but a variety of them to ward off insects. These compounds act in various ways both outside and inside the insect. Plants have been interacting with insects for millions of years and have adapted multiple modes of action or physiological pathways to reduce insect damage. For example, wild parsnip (*Pastinaca sativa*) produces chemicals from at least seven different pathways. Allelochemicals may also interact with each other to increase effectiveness. *Umbelliferous plants*, a group of plants that includes parsnip and carrot, produce an allelochemical that amplifies the toxicity of another allelochemical, making it five times as toxic to corn earworm.

Insect defenses against allelochemicals

Herbivorous insects cope with allelochemicals through a variety of mechanisms, because in a sense, they are being poisoned when they feed. They may rapidly excrete these unwanted compounds, degrade them with enzymes, or otherwise neutralize them before they reach toxic levels.

The tobacco hornworm (*Manduca sexta*), a common pest of tomatoes in the garden, is an insect that rapidly excretes allelochemicals. It feeds on host plants that contain nicotine (which is very toxic to many insects and other animals) and other alkaloids, and then it excretes them before accumulating a toxic dose. Nicotine is toxic to animal nervous systems, but hornworms are able to prevent it from entering the nervous system by filtering it out of the blood and excreting it.

Another way that insects deal with allelochemicals is to degrade them (break them down) with enzymes. Within minutes of toxin ingestion, there is a dramatic increase in the level of neutralizing enzymes, measured to be as much as forty-five times higher than normal. Once enzymes have broken down the allelochemical, the insect can digest or excrete the breakdown products. As soon as the allelochemical is no longer present, enzyme activity begins to drop. Thus, an insect may possess a variety of enzymes effective against specific toxins. It can produce them rapidly as needed, but it does not have to use its energy and resources to maintain them at a constant high level.

Mollusks

Slugs and snails are not very closely related to insects. They are *mollusks*: animals protected by a calcium-rich shell or that have remnants of a shell. Mollusks also include clams, squids, and octopi. In fact, the physiology of slugs and snails is different enough from that of insects that insecticides do not control them. *Slugs* are snails without shells. The snails and slugs that are garden pests have lungs and breathe air and also can breathe through their skin. They have no legs but rather glide along on a muscular surface called a *foot*.

By producing large amounts of mucus, slugs and snails are actually able to crawl along the edge of a razor blade without being harmed. The mucus trails that they leave during the night appear as silvery ribbons in the morning sunlight across the leaves of attacked plants. Plate 59 shows a gray garden slug (*Agriolimax reticulates*) with its mucus trail. These trails usually dry up and disappear by mid-morning.

Slugs and snails are very susceptible to water loss, and the mucus undoubtedly helps to prevent it. Because these mollusks need a constant supply of moisture, they are found in high numbers in shady areas where soil moisture is retained due to closely spaced plants or mulches. They climb plants and feed primarily at night when the humidity is high.

Slugs and snails feed with a finely toothed tongue-like structure called a *radula*, which scrapes through the surface of the leaf. Eventually, a hole is eaten through the leaf. Whereas most chewing insects feed at the leaf margin, slugs and snails tend to feed in the center of the leaf, leaving a hole with undamaged leaf tissue around it. Leaves with heavy damage have many circular to angular holes at the leaf center but little or no feeding damage along the margins. By contrast, insect-damaged leaves typically have heavy feeding along the margins but few or no holes at the center.

Slugs and snails most often attack hosta (as shown in plate 60), violet, impatiens, and other thin-leaved plants. This may be because shade-adapted plants tend to have thin leaves and grow where slugs and snails are numerous (rather than that the slugs and snails are attracted to their thin leaves). Indeed, slugs and snails feed heavily on cabbage and broccoli—whose leaves are thick and have a very heavy waxy covering—if they are placed close together in shady areas.

Chapter 4

Recognizing and Assessing
Pest Problems

With IPM it is critical, although not always easy, to identify the pest responsible for causing plant damage—be it an insect, mite, mollusk, or disease. For example, holes in leaves may be caused by late frost damage, by chewing *insects*, or by a foliar disease. Pest identification is important because some insects and diseases are more damaging than others and because many problems produce similar symptoms. Once you know what kind of pest is present, you can better judge whether the potential damage justifies management.

Insect and mite feeding types

As we discussed in chapter 3, insects and mites that attack plants in landscapes feed in various ways. The five major feeding behaviors are chewing, sucking, mining, boring, and galling. Chewing insects such as beetles, caterpillars, grasshoppers, earwigs, and weevils—shown in plates 61 through 66—physically remove portions of plants including leaves, or consume entire plants.

Sucking insects or mites such as aphids, whiteflies, mealybugs, scales, thrips, leafhoppers, and spider mites—shown in plates 67 through 77—possess piercing-sucking mouthparts that they insert into the plant to remove fluids. They generally cause plant stunting or wilting. In addition, many sucking insects transmit plant viruses—such as impatiens necrotic spot virus (tospovirus), shown in plate 78—or phytoplasmas that may be extremely harmful to landscape plants.

78

Mining insects (leafminers), which include beetles, caterpillars, wasps, and flies, create tunnels—as shown on the leaf of a columbine (*Aquilegia*) in plate 79—or blotches on plant leaves or stems as they feed below the leaf surface and within the plant tissues.

Wood-boring insects such as beetles (the bronze birch borer shown in plate 80 is an example), caterpillars, and wasps feed within the water and food-conducting portions of plants. They can cause plant stunting, wilting, and possibly death. Plate 81 shows tunneling damage to a young cedar caused by wood-boring insect larvae.

Galling insects or mites—which include aphids, thrips, eriophyid mites, psyllids, midges, adelgids, and cynipid gall wasps (shown in plates 82 through 88)—exist inside of plants and create outgrowths on leaves and branches. Generally speaking, insect and mite galls are not harmful to plants; however, there are fungal galls that can be damaging.

Feeding behavior is critical for some IPM options. Because chewers, miners, and suckers are exposed, they are generally easier to manage with pest control materials such as insecticides. These insects and mites also are more susceptible to natural enemies such as parasitic wasps and predators. Plate 89 shows aphids exposed to natural enemies; and plate 90 shows parasitized aphids. In plate 91, the leafminer larvae tunneling in a verbena leaf are restricted within the leaf tissue and are susceptible to natural enemies—particularly parasitoids that use the difference in light reflected from the damaged and undamaged portions of the leaf to locate the larvae. In contrast, borers and gallmakers are protected within the plant, which makes control more difficult.

Insect leftovers

The best way to ensure an accurate diagnosis of an insect problem on plants grown in landscapes and gardens is to see the organism causing the problem. At times, however, we have no choice but to rely on "insect leftovers"—subtle reminders or remains that indicate the insects' presence. Most insect leftovers are a direct result of feeding on plants; however, insects also may leave evidence from the normal process of molting (shedding of old outer skin, shown in plate 92), as a result of increasing in size or changing into another life form. For example, aphids leave white cast skins as evidence of molting, as shown in plate 93. These cast skins are sometimes misidentified as whiteflies or dead aphids.

Honeydew

Many insects with piercing-sucking mouthparts—including aphids, whiteflies, soft scales, and mealybugs—produce a clear, sticky liquid called *honeydew* (shown on the leaf of *Ficus* in plate 94), which provides evidence of their presence. These groups of insects sometimes produce honeydew in large quantities because they require protein, in the form of amino acids, for development and reproduction. To obtain those amino acids, the insects must consume large amounts of plant sap, which contains an assortment of other materials in larger quantities than amino acids. The insects then excrete the excess as honeydew.

Honeydew may be a problem for several reasons:

- It attracts insects wasps, hornets, and yellow jackets, which may increase the likelihood of people getting stung.
- It attracts carpenter ants (*Camponotus*) and other ant species, which protect piercing-sucking insects from natural enemies such as parasitoids (parasitic wasps) and predators.
- It is an excellent growing medium for black sooty mold fungi (*Capnodium*), shown on southern yew (*Podocarpus macrophyllus*) in plate 95, which may reduce the plant's ability to manufacture food and are aesthetically unappealing.

Frass deposits

Chewing insects, particularly caterpillars, may leave evidence of their presence in the form of frass deposits (fecal material or other debris). This is the excess, similar to the honeydew of piercing-sucking insects, that caterpillars excrete as a result of consuming more than they can use. For example, a single gypsy moth (*Lymantria dispar*) caterpillar—shown in plate 96—can eat one square foot of leaf material per day, which results in the production of tremendous amounts of frass.

Some insects leave black, hardened fecal deposits on the underside of leaves (as shown in plate 97). This type of insect leftover is characteristic of lace bugs and thrips and therefore helps in their identification.

Many wood-boring insects leave very noticeable leftovers when they infest a plant—either when the larvae tunnel within the plant, or when adults use their chewing mouthparts to create emergence holes. An excellent way to determine if wood-boring insects are the problem is to look for sawdust-like deposits or "wood shavings" at the base of plants or below entry/exit sites. For example, Zimmerman pine moth larval tunneling produces frass deposits that are visible at or near the base of the infested tree.

Insect distribution and abundance

Before making an IPM decision, it is also important to understand how plant-feeding insects or mites are distributed and how abundant they are. Rarely do plant-feeding insects and mites attack every plant in a landscape; rather, they tend to prefer certain plant types over others. By mapping pest populations in a landscape, we can establish which areas are more heavily infested. This makes it possible to spot treat insect and mite populations, as opposed to conducting wide-scale applications of pest control materials. Spot treating also helps to preserve existing natural enemies.

Usually, insect and mite populations in landscapes and gardens are distributed on plants in clumps or aggregations rather than uniformly. Clumped distributions result from grouping behavior or feeding in particular habitat patches. Examples of clumped distributions include aphids feeding on new growth; scales located on older growth; Japanese beetles located on exposed, sunny foliage; and white grubs in open, mowed areas.

Reproductive capacity or *potential natality*, defined as the reproductive rate of individuals in an optimum environment, is what primarily determines the abundance of insects or mites in home landscapes. Insect and mite numbers may vary temporally (in time) or spatially (in space) depending on factors such as temperature, season, plant types grown, presence of natural enemies, and movement into an area (immigration) or out of an area (emigration).

Pest activity varies with the season; however, the highest level of activity occurs primarily during spring and summer when the weather is warmer and plants are leafed out. Knowing the number of pests present can help to estimate their impact and determine whether or not there is sufficient cause to spend time and money on management. For example, ten to twenty Japanese beetle grubs per square foot are enough to cause injury to turfgrass (shown in plate 98); therefore, scouting for grubs in turf can help prevent serious damage.

The amount of plant damage that insect and mite pests cause also may depend on factors such as

- *Rate of reproduction and length of generation (from egg to adult).* For example, aphids and spider mites are major landscape and garden pests because they have very high reproductive rates and short generation times.
- *Number of generations.* Some caterpillar species, such as mimosa webworm (*Homadaula anisocentra*) and black cutworm, have two generations per year, whereas others, such as eastern tent caterpillar (*Malacosoma americanum*) and gypsy moth, have one generation per year. Caterpillars with two generations per year may cause more plant damage over a longer period of time.
- *Number of eggs laid.* For example, cecropia moth females lay only a few eggs, whereas gypsy moth females can lay more than 500 eggs.

Determining the impact of pests on plants

TNSL, which stands for timing, number, stage, and location, is an approach to assessing pest problems and determining their potential impact on plants.

Timing

A pest may attack a plant early-season, mid-season, or late-season, and this timing determines the potential impact on plant health and whether the plant will recover. For example, eastern tent caterpillars (shown in plates 99 and 100), cankerworms, and gypsy moths are early-season defoliators of many deciduous trees and shrubs. The larvae feed on leaves as they emerge, and this significantly impacts plant health because trees and shrubs are unable to photosynthesize or manufacture food without leaves. This type of injury warrants the use of an IPM strategy to minimize plant stress and ensure survival.

By contrast, subsequent generations of fall webworm (*Hyphantria cunea*, shown in plates 101 and 102), yellownecked caterpillar, and mimosa webworm attack trees and shrubs later in the season—a time when plants are getting ready to shed their leaves and are allocating minimal resources toward growth. As a result, the impact of larvae feeding is low, and it may be advisable to do nothing or to simply prune.

The apple scab fungus is a common defoliator of landscape crabapples. Most infection occurs in spring when temperatures are moderate, humidity is high, and plant tissues are succulent. Although additional infection may occur throughout summer, the hardened foliage resists attack and the environment is usually less conducive in midsummer. Therefore, the best time to manage apple scab is during the initial infection period in spring.

Number

The quantity of individuals present in a population may be high, medium, or low. These are subjective terms, and their meaning will depend on your own interpretation and the time of year. A high pest population on a plant generally warrants some type of IPM strategy, particularly if the pest has high reproductive capabilities (more individuals produced), such as aphids. Such cases may warrant greater use of a pest control material or more frequent use of hard water sprays. Medium or low pest populations may be of no concern initially, other than that, depending on the particular pest, they may develop into a high pest population. The numbers may have minimal impact on plant health, and they may be easier to manage with natural enemies, thus less likely to require pest control materials.

Conversely, even low numbers of insect borers, such as the bronze birch borer and the ash/lilac borer, can cause heavy damage. In addition, low numbers of bagworms (*Thyridopteryx ephemeraeformis*) can cause heavy damage to needled evergreens. When dealing with these insects, any evidence of infestation may warrant control efforts.

Stage

The age of a plant or its stage of development can be either small (young) or mature (old). In general, small or young plants are more susceptible to lower pest numbers than mature or older plants, and their plant health is more likely to be compromised. For example, fewer than fifty aphids may have greater impact on young trees or shrubs than the same number on a mature tree or shrub. An infestation of one or two wood-boring insects may be more

Prevention is the best defense

Most IPM disease control options stress prevention. A pathogen is difficult to eradicate once present on a plant, and some diseases can be very damaging if left unchecked. For example, black spot of rose, botrytis blight on bedding plants, Dutch elm disease, fire blight, and aster yellows must be contained at the first sign of disease because plants may quickly become unappealing, weakened, and even die.

detrimental to the health of a young tree than to an older tree. This information helps to determine whether or not the use of a pest control material is warranted.

Root diseases are a much greater problem for seedlings or transplants than they are for mature trees. Rhizoctonia root rot and pythium root rot may kill bedding transplants if left unchecked, whereas mature plants may be able to avoid infection or may exhibit limited injury. On the other hand, young plants may be able to deal with verticillium wilt, wood rots, and fusarium wilt, whereas older plants may be more susceptible to them.

Location

Landscape or garden plants may be located in areas of high visibility or heavy use (such as close to pedestrian traffic or near structures, as in figure 10), or in the less visible background. Pest problems, regardless of severity, are more likely to be noticed on highly visible plants, and as a result, these plants are more likely to receive higher pest management inputs. Plants in the background of a landscape or garden—usually shrubs or trees—are not observed closely on a regular basis. As a result, pest management inputs may be minimal.

Evaluating pest populations

The key to knowing when to implement a pest management strategy and to determining the effectiveness of an IPM program is to monitor pest populations regularly. For insects and mites, monitoring involves detecting pest pop-

Figure 10. The health of landscape plants is more obvious if the plants are close to pedestrian traffic. Photo courtesy of Raymond A. Cloyd

Less is sometimes more

A pest population is seldom noticed on background plants until damage or injury is apparent. Although this translates into the reduced input of any pest management strategy, especially the use of a pest control material, it is not necessarily a bad thing. Without intervention, natural enemies have the opportunity to manage a pest population before numbers reach damaging levels.

This holds true for diseased plants in the landscape as well. For example, pine trees infected with sphaeropsis tip blight along a windbreak may require only sanitation methods to maintain acceptable trees. However, the same tree in a focal point of the landscape may require applications of preventive fungicides along with pruning of surrounding plants to promote better air flow.

Figure 11. Visual inspection of a leaf underside for pests. Photo courtesy of Raymond A. Cloyd

ulations with a trapping device, through visual inspection (as shown in figure 11), or by both means. A 10-power hand lens is useful for identifying small insects.

The most practical method of scouting in home landscapes is to inspect plant parts for the presence of insects, mites, or diseases. This includes checking leaf undersides, terminal shoots, buds, and flowers. For example, inspecting landscapes routinely will help to detect eastern tent caterpillar egg masses in winter, stem cankers in early spring, and the egg masses of squash bugs, pine aphids, and gypsy moth.

Another way to *assess* insects or mites is to use traps. Pitfall traps, like the one shown in figure 13, passively capture insects that stumble across them, such as adult black vine weevil (*Otiorhynchus sulcatus*). Alternatively, you can place disposable cups or cans in holes in the ground that are of the same depth as the cup. Adult black vine weevils and adult billbugs inadvertently fall into the cups and become trapped because they are unable to fly or crawl out. To scout and help time applications of pest control materials for scales, wrap double-sided sticky tape around scale-infested branches or twigs. When the crawlers emerge and start moving around, they become stuck on the tape. By examining the tape regularly, you can determine when the scales are in the crawler stage, which is most susceptible to control.

Monitoring greenhouse insect populations

Yellow sticky cards, like the one shown in figure 12, are trapping devices that are placed above or within the plant canopy. More useful in greenhouses or conservatories than in landscapes and gardens, the sticky cards attract flying insects such as moths, beetles, thrips, and whiteflies. In addition, sticky cards capture natural enemies such as parasitic wasps (that is, parasitoids) and predatory beetles. Sticky cards need to be checked weekly.

Figure 12. Yellow sticky card used to monitor winged insects, including thrips, whiteflies, leafminers, beetles, and moths. Photo courtesy of Raymond A. Cloyd

How to monitor for spider mites

An efficient way to monitor for spider mites is to shake a branch over a white letter-sized sheet of paper. Any spider mites that are present will fall off, land on the paper, and crawl around. You can than crush the collected mites to determine if they are a pest or are beneficial: Plant-feeding spider mites produce a green streak when crushed, whereas predatory mites produce an orange-red streak.

Figure 13. Pitfall trap used to capture insects that walk on the soil surface. Photo courtesy of Raymond A. Cloyd

Attracting insects to traps

Many traps are attractive to insects. The traps that are general attractants, such as light traps, are of limited use for home landscapes. However, species-specific or group-specific traps are available for many insects that attack trees and shrubs in landscapes. The majority of these specific traps use compounds called *pheromones*, which are derived from chemicals produced by insects that act as sexual attractants or modify insect behavior in some way. Pheromone traps can be useful for monitoring insect flights, by providing clues to when insects are laying eggs or the eggs are hatching. This information is important for properly timing applications of pest control materials.

Different shapes of pheromone traps are used to attract different insects. Two pests that are effectively monitored using pheromone traps are the Zimmerman pine moth, and the ash/lilac borer. Figure 14 shows a pheromone trap for Zimmerman pine moth.

Figure 14. Pheromone trap used to capture adult male Zimmerman pine moths, to help time the application of pest control materials. Photo courtesy of Raymond A. Cloyd

Evaluating plant diseases

When working with field crops, there are many evaluative monitoring scales and keys available for assessing plant diseases. When working in a landscape situation where there is a heterogeneous *mix* of plants, however, such scales

Beware the Japanese beetle trap

Not all insect traps are useful. Japanese beetle traps capture many Japanese beetle adults, but they also lure more of them into the landscape or garden than would be present without the traps, thus leading to increased plant damage. In addition, Japanese beetle adults may feed on plants before being trapped and raise the potential for more grubs (Japanese beetle larvae) during late summer and fall. High numbers of grubs feeding on turfgrass roots may lead to excessive damage.

and keys are inappropriate. The most useful monitoring tool for plant diseases in the landscape is visual plant inspection.

Successful diagnosis of plant disease relies on symptoms and signs of the pathogen. *Symptoms* of plant disease include all visible clues that there is something abnormal about the plant. Of course, to be able to recognize an abnormality in a plant, we need to know about the qualities of a normal plant. For example, should leaves be variegated, or is that a symptom of viral infection? Comparisons with similar plant species in the area are helpful in determining what is normal. Symptoms of infectious diseases include:

- Fungal pathogens can cause leaf spots, blights, wilting, galls, root rot, cankers, and fruit rots.
- Bacterial pathogens can cause leaf spots, blights, cankers, wilting, soft rot, and galls, some of which resemble fungal symptoms.
- Viral pathogens can cause chlorosis, odd color patterns or mosaics on the foliage, or distorted or stunted growth.
- Phytoplasmas also cause stunting, chlorosis, and odd growth patterns.

Noninfectious diseases also can produce some of these symptoms. For example, yellowing of tree foliage could be the result of a phytoplasma, or it could be related to iron deficiency, soil pH imbalance, flooded conditions, damage to the base of the tree, or another physical problem. Thus, symptoms often provide only a clue to the actual cause or causes of the problem.

Signs of plant disease are the actual parts of the pathogen that occur on or near the infected plant. Most signs of disease involve fungal pathogens, and these important clues often provide critical information when diagnosing a plant disease. Fungal pathogens may produce spores, mycelia, fruiting bodies, or other fungal structures that may be visible clues to the presence of a disease. The rust and powdery mildew diseases form spores that are visible on leaves, stems, or fruit. When spores of these fungi accompany symptoms of yellowing and poor growth, disease is clearly implicated as part of the problem. Fungi also may produce mycelia as clues. Armillaria root rot affects many species of trees, particularly oaks. White, fan-like mycelia of the fungus may be visible growing between the bark and wood at the base of the tree. Often rhizomorphs, shoestring-like masses of mycelia, are visible in the same area. In some cases, *Armillaria* also produce distinctive mushrooms around infected trees. The mycelia, the rhizomorphs, and the mushrooms are all signs of the disease.

Although most signs of plant disease involve fungal pathogens, and although individual bacterial cells cannot be seen with the naked eye, masses of bacteria may be visible as exudates or slime. This is the case with bacterial soft rot and the exudates sometimes seen with fire blight on ornamental plants.

A few other general facts are helpful in disease diagnosis:

- Diseases tend to start at a focal point where the initial infection took place and spread from that point. Therefore, it is helpful to note the pattern of the problem in the landscape.
- Most disease pathogens are also rather host specific. Hollyhock rust (*Puccinia malvacearum*) will not infect hostas or crabapples. The presence of anthracnose on oaks in a landscape does not mean it will also appear on dogwood.
- Diseases usually develop rather slowly. Ideal conditions can speed up the disease process, but diseases do not appear overnight on landscape plants. The sudden appearance of plant disease is more likely the result of infrequent plant inspection.

Good reference books on insects, mites, and diseases—such as those listed in appendix A—are invaluable in diagnosis. Most are organized either by host plant or by specific pests. When a plant appears abnormal, use these books to research what sorts of problems might affect that host, then study the plant for evidence that may confirm the cause of the problem. Look closely for all factors that might possibly cause the problems at hand. It is very likely that more than one factor is involved. Consider using both trapping and visual inspection to determine the effectiveness of any management options you use to deal with insects, mites, or diseases in the landscape and garden.

Chapter 5

Cultural Pest Management

Plant culture—that is, how plants are grown and maintained in the garden and landscape—can make a difference in the types of pests present and their numbers. The attractiveness of plants to pests can be affected by the species and varieties of plants, where they are planted, and when they are planted, watered, fertilized, and harvested. Thus, the best way to prevent pest problems in the first place is to strive for good cultural practices.

Host plant susceptibility and resistance

Some plants are less susceptible to injury from pests than others. For example, some tomato varieties are listed as *VFNT resistant* (see figure 15), meaning that they are less susceptible to verticillium wilt, fusarium wilt, nematodes, and tobacco mosaic virus. This type of resistance came about through selective breeding of plants that showed resistance with plants that produced abundant and high quality fruit.

Resistance is the ability of a plant to avoid damage by a pest, and susceptibility is the likelihood that a plant will be damaged by a pest. Resistance tends to imply that a pathogen or insect pest can attack a plant in large numbers and in any growing conditions, and yet no harm will come to the plant. In reality, total resistance is uncommon. It is helpful to think of resistance and susceptibility as a continuum—from plants that are almost never damaged to plants that are devastated by pests in any growing situation. Between these

92

Figure 15. Tomato seed packets listing disease resistance. Photo courtesy of Philip L. Nixon

two extremes are many intermediate levels of susceptibility. Susceptibility is dependent not only on the plant's genetic makeup, but also on other factors such as growing conditions and level of pest pressure.

As we discussed in chapter 3, allelochemicals, or secondary plant compounds, are chemicals that a plant produces that make it less attractive to a pest or may actually be toxic to the pest. A plant produces allelochemicals in addition to the chemicals more necessary for basic growth and development. When a plant is coping with drought, incorrect lighting, poor soils, and other conditions that are much less than ideal, it produces fewer secondary plant compounds. Because these compounds are not absolutely necessary, they are

The concern about genetic engineering

Genetic engineering is the technological process that purposefully changes an organism's genes or the expression of the organism's genes. It can move genes that produce desired traits into plants, resulting in the production of *genetically modified organisms (GMOs)*. The use of high technology and speed with which GMOs are developed, as well as the combining of traits from unrelated organisms, is alarming to many people. Despite analyzing and testing of GMOs, including feeding studies, much of the public has a high level of concern. To many, the notion of creating new plant characteristics in a garden or greenhouse is much more comforting than their production in a laboratory.

easily eliminated for the survival of the plant. As a result, plants in poor grow-ing conditions tend to be more susceptible to pathogens and insect pests.

Numerous diseases, such as canker diseases, verticillium wilt (shown on a red maple tree in plate 103), wood rots, and botrytis blight, are found pri-marily on plants or plant parts that are in decline due to environmental rea-sons such as inadequate light, fertility, or pH. Many of these organisms are pri-marily *saprophytic*—meaning that they grow on dead plant material—but will attack plants in poor health. Growing plants suitable to the hardiness zone, with sufficient space and proper light, and in soil with appropriate fertility and moisture will provide an excellent defense against such diseases.

Reduced host plant susceptibility

A plant and its pests evolve together. That is, as the plant or pest acquires an advantage over the other, traits evolve to counteract it. This process, called coevolution, leads to host plant resistance, or more correctly, reduced host plant susceptibility. The three main categories of reduced host plant suscep-tibility are antixenosis, antibiosis, and tolerance.

Antixenosis

The first category of reduced host plant susceptibility, antixenosis, refers to the relationship of plants with characteristics that make them less attractive to a pest or less hospitable to a pathogen and therefore less likely to be attacked. This is commonly called nonpreference because the pest, typically an insect, avoids the plant or prefers not to attack it. For example, the plant may have characteristics that make it less attractive to an insect or other pest for food, egg-laying, or shelter. Alternatively, the plant may lack the struc-ture or nutrient value necessary for a pathogen to be very successful in infect-ing the plant, or chemicals on the plant's surface may repel a fungus or other pathogen.

Often, plants have physical characteristics that reduce attack by insects and other animals. For example, the leaves may have a thick waxy covering that is hard to penetrate. And when leaves and stems are covered with tri-chomes (hair-like structures) that are long and numerous, it becomes diffi-cult for small pests such as mites and thrips to reach the actual leaf surface to feed. The trichomes may produce sticky compounds that make it difficult for insects and mites to move around on the plant. Thorns, which are an extreme example of surface growths on a plant, reduce feeding by herbivorous mammals.

Plants also can have physical characteristics that reduce their susceptibility to diseases. For example, some plants have a thick waxy coating or thick cuticle that helps prevent invasion by bacteria and fungi. Small openings of the stomata and lenticels or a hairy leaf also may serve as a protective mechanism. Even the size of xylem vessels may be a factor affecting infection by a pathogen, as with Dutch elm disease. Quick plugging of the xylem is a resist-

How plant odors affect pests

Some plants produce odors or other chemicals that repel attacking pests. Conversely, plants may not produce certain odors or other chemicals that insects and other pests associate with an appropriate food source. This in part has led to the idea of companion planting in the garden. Popular literature abounds with suggestions that planting garlic (*Allium*), tansy (*Tanacetum*), nasturtium (*Tropaeolum*), marigold, catnip (*Nepeta cataria*), or other plants near garden plants will repel insect pests. Although the repellency of certain plant odors to certain insects has been documented, research under field conditions has shown repeatedly that companion planting typically fails to increase yields or quality of produce.

Insects commonly use plant odors to locate host plants. At least twenty-nine species of true bugs, beetles, flies, butterflies, and moths have been shown to use plant odors to find their host plants, and the actual number of insects attracted to plant odors is probably much higher. These insects evolved to find host plants by odor, sight, and other means in a natural world where host plants are typically surrounded by nonhost plants, some of which produce insect repellent odors.

Research has shown that companion plants need to be very numerous and close to the host plant to be effective. In these situations, the companion plants shade out and compete for nutrients and water with the host plant to such a degree that produce production is typically equal to or less than that of plants spaced properly and more exposed to insect pests.

ance mechanism that the tree uses against the Dutch elm disease fungus. And because shorter, smaller diameter vessels are easier for the tree to plug, this anatomic characteristic is an important defense against disease.

If plant cells do not provide the food needs of a fungus, the fungus will not infect. For example, the fungal pathogens *Rhizoctonia* and *Venturia inaequalis* (apple scab fungus) need certain growth factors to infect a host plant. The absence of these growth factors in the host prevents infection by the fungus.

Antibiosis

The second category of reduced host plant susceptibility, antibiosis, refers to the relationship of plants that produce chemicals which are harmful to a pest or pathogen. These chemicals may reduce the ability of a pathogen or insect pest to reproduce or to grow properly. Latex is a material produced by milkweeds (*Asclepias*) and other plants that physically plugs insect mouthparts, making it difficult for insects to continue feeding. Alkaloids produced by milkweeds, nicotine produced by tobacco (*Nicotiana*), and tannins produced by oaks are all examples of chemicals that can harm attacking insects.

Plants also have structural and biochemical defense mechanisms to use in defense against pathogens. One such mechanism involves recognizing the presence of a pathogen through detection of substances that various pathogens release (such as carbohydrates and fatty acids) when they contact the host plant. How quickly the host recognizes the pathogen and initiates defense reactions will determine its ability to fight the infection. The host uses chemical signals to inform cell proteins and genes to begin defense reactions against the pathogen. Even some synthetic chemicals can activate this signaling system to protect the host from the pathogen.

Considering all the spores and bacteria that inadvertently fall on plants and how few diseases actually result from these chance happenings, other defenses must be involved. The host plant produces its own set of toxins to fight pathogens. These toxins, which may have strong antifungal or antimicrobial activity, are involved in activities from preventing spore germination to breaking down the chitin in the cell wall of a fungus. Plants able to produce chitinase are often resistant to the fungal root rot pathogen *Rhizoctonia solani*. There are also chemicals toxic to fungi that plants can release on their surface, often promoted by the presence of a film of water. Tomatoes release a chemical that is toxic to *Botrytis*, a fungus that can cause extensive foliar blight.

Other inhibitors (such as phenolic compounds and tannins) are present within the cell, some of which may actually counteract the pectin-degrading (pectolytic) enzymes of certain pathogens. When the fungus attacks with these enzymes, the plant counters with a wave of inhibiting compounds. Some cells on the surface of the plant even have enzymes to break down the cell wall of a pathogen. Thus, as the fungus uses its enzymes to break down the plant cell wall, the plant uses its own enzymes to break down the fungal cell wall.

Even when a pathogen has found its way inside the host plant, the host has various defense reactions at its disposal, including structural reactions to the pathogen involving the cell wall and membranes. In some cases, the cytoplasm can surround and isolate bacterial pathogens.

Some fescue (*Festuca*) and rye (*Elymus*) turfgrasses contain *endophytes*— symbiotic fungi that occur naturally. A *symbiotic* relationship is one in which two organisms live together for the benefit of each. In this situation, the fungi have a place to live within the grass, and the fungi produce toxins that control the plant's pests. Endophytes pass from generation to generation in the grass seed. Very common in the stems and leaves, endophytes effectively reduce the numbers of aboveground feeding insects such as sod webworms (shown in plate 104), cutworms, chinch bugs, greenbugs (*Schizaphis graminum*), and billbugs. Because endophytes are not numerous in the root system, white grubs and other belowground feeding insects are not eliminated. Genetic engineering efforts are underway to transfer endophytes to Kentucky bluegrass and other turfgrass species where the endophytes do not occur naturally.

Tolerance

The third category of reduced host plant susceptibility, *tolerance*, describes plants that are able to grow and reproduce when attacked by diseases and insect pests to a degree that would otherwise severely harm or kill related plants. These plants are able to tolerate the attack.

Feeding damage to garden beans from adult bean leaf beetles (*Cerotoma trifurcata*), adult Japanese beetles, woollybear caterpillars, and grasshoppers can be severe, yet the production of beans may not be affected. Plate 105 shows leaf damage to snap beans caused by adult bean leaf beetles. Trees and shrubs are fed upon by many species of caterpillars, beetles, and sucking insects—and despite damage, the plants continue to grow and thrive.

Possibly in response to mechanical force, plants attacked by pathogens often produce structures within the cells called papillae. *Papillae* are intracellular protuberances of the cell wall that may slow fungal spread. Plants that are invaded by fungi, viruses, or nematodes may develop swollen, distorted, or otherwise modified cell walls. Such changes may provide localized protection from toxins produced by a pathogen. For example, the formation of a cork layer around an infection site isolates that site and keeps the pathogen from spreading. Apple scab (*Venturia inaequalis*) lesions on the fruit have this corky layer.

Plants often form an abscission layer in response to infection by fungi, bacteria, or viruses, and this causes infected leaves to drop. This is the case with the bacterial leaf spots of ornamental *Prunus* species. Rose leaves infected with black spot produce large quantities of ethylene, which is thought to cause leaf abscission.

Fungal spores and bacteria can spread rapidly in the xylem tissues. Plants resistant to the pathogens produce overgrowths of parenchyma as well as gums in response to attack. As a result, the vascular system becomes plugged, which prevents pathogen spread at the expense of the localized area that is plugged. Resistant species are able to plug such vessels quickly, whereas susceptible species cannot plug the xylem quickly enough to stop infection. Some pathogens, such as the Dutch elm disease fungus, may produce chemicals that slow this plant defense mechanism, allowing infection to spread before the xylem is plugged.

The production of gums around infection sites is another plant response that effectively walls off the fungus from the rest of the plant. An example would be gum formation when infections occur on ornamental stone fruits such as ornamental cherry and plum (*Prunus*). Stem cankers are usually accompanied by gum formation.

A final example is the hypersensitive reaction to inoculation from a pathogen. This results in rapid death of all cell membranes that the pathogen contacts, leading to the production of resin-like granules in the cytoplasm, which trap the pathogen. Sudden tissue death of this sort prevents further spread of the disease within the plant.

Coevolution

Reduced host plant susceptibility is frequently the result of two or all three of the mechanisms just discussed—antixenosis, antibiosis, and tolerance—and may be the result of more than one factor within each mechanism. Because diseases and insect pests counteract traits that reduce plant susceptibility to them, the interaction between the host and the pest is constantly changing. As the host or pest changes slightly to gain the advantage, the other responds or evolves to counteract the advantage.

This too is illustrated with Dutch elm disease: Shorter, smaller diameter vessels that are easier to plug reduce the effect of the pathogen on the plant. However, the Dutch elm disease fungus may produce chemicals that slow this defense mechanism of the plant, allowing infection to spread before the xylem is plugged. This evolving on the one hand and then evolving in response is called *coevolution* or *adaptive radiation*.

Coevolution can continue for a group of pests and plants until the plants are attacked very little or not at all by most pests. There are a few species of caterpillars and aphids that successfully attack cabbage, broccoli, brussels sprouts, kale, and other *Brassica* plants (cole crops), but other caterpillars, beetles, and many other pests are unable to attack these plants. Hornworms (*Manduca*), cutworms, armyworms, blister beetles, flea beetles, Colorado potato beetle, and aphids are able to attack various solanaceous plants (plants in the nightshade family, such as tomato, potato, tobacco, pepper, and eggplant), but many insect pests do not attack these plants.

Among closely related plants, for example cucurbit crops (plants in the squash family), some species and varieties may be highly susceptible, whereas other species and varieties may have relatively low susceptibility. The squash vine borer severely attacks zucchini but does not severely attack summer (crookneck), pattypan, scallopini, and other summer squash varieties. It also severely attacks some winter squash—including acorn, delicata, and hubbard—but not butternut squash. Plate 106 shows damage from this insect, which may infest susceptible squashes so heavily that the main stem separates from the ground. On the other hand, vining varieties that are encouraged to root off the vines will continue to produce squash through the season—an example of tolerance.

Iris borer (*Macronoctua onusta*) more commonly attacks tall bearded irises than other iris varieties and species. However, tall bearded irises have large rhizomes that are able to tolerate a considerable amount of feeding by this insect. Plate 107 shows iris borer larvae feeding on the rhizome of a tall bearded iris. Although less susceptible to iris borer attack, Japanese (*Iris sanguinea*), Louisiana, Siberian (*I. sibirica*), and other irises with small rhizomes are more likely to be severely damaged or killed by an infestation.

Bronze birch borer attacks many species of white barked birches, but rarely attacks river birch (*Betula nigra*) and Whitespire birch (*B. platyphylla* var. *japonica* 'Whitespire'). Honeysuckle aphid damages Zabelii honeysuckle (*Lonicera tatarica* 'Zabelii') severely, but does not damage Arnold Red honeysuckle (*L. tatarica* 'Arnold Red') and most other honeysuckle varieties and species.

Mowing and pruning for plant health

Chapter 6 discusses the importance of mowing and pruning to remove weeds, diseases, and insect pests. In this section, we will discuss their importance in effective cultural management practices.

Mowing

Weeds become established in lawns by taking advantage of bare soil between grass plants. When lawns are mowed properly on a regular basis, the number of grass plants per unit area is increased, thus eliminating most areas of bare soil where weeds can grow. The result is a lawn with few weeds.

Although grasses will tolerate close mowing, it is stressful to them and increases their susceptibility to many diseases. Mowing higher results in healthier turf (although very tall turf is more susceptible to some diseases such as snow mold). Mowing frequently, so that no more than one-third of the grass blade is removed, also results in healthier turf.

Turf that is consistently mowed higher, at 3 inches or more, will shade out low-growing weeds, such as the dandelions shown in plate 108. With high mowing for several years, weeds such as dandelions usually disappear gradually, except at turf edges such as along driveways and sidewalks where they receive enough light to survive.

Pruning

The proper pruning of trees and shrubs also can prevent pests. Wood rots, cankers, and other diseases of trees and shrubs are common on dead and dying branches. As a tree or shrub matures, higher branches shade out lower branches, causing them to die. Disease pathogens, bark beetles, and other borers attack this dead wood. Pruning out dead wood not only improves the appearance of the plant, but also removes disease inoculum and borers that can attack nearby plants or other areas of the same plant. For disease control, we strongly recommend removing dead wood from landscape trees before spring growth begins.

The timing of pruning is also important. For example, borer adults, particularly moth borers, lay their eggs at the edge of pruning and other wounds. Clearwing moth borers such as ash/lilac borer, dogwood borer, viburnum borer, and peachtree borer are usually present as egg-laying adults in late spring to midsummer. Therefore, it is best to delay pruning of susceptible plants until late summer when the moths have ceased flying. This should help reduce attack, because pruning wounds will have time to close and heal before borer adults are out again laying eggs.

Although the bronze birch borer is a beetle that can chew its own egg-laying niche, adults are attracted to freshly wounded trees. Therefore, avoid pruning birches in spring when egg-laying is taking place. And because the oak wilt fungus spreads by bark beetles attracted to the sap of infected trees, it is best to prune oaks when sap is not flowing, such as during the winter, to avoid the spread of disease to healthy trees.

Transplanted tree and shrub care

Because transplanting is traumatic for plants, extra protection from diseases and insect borers is important with newly transplanted trees and shrubs. Typically with field-dug trees and shrubs, much of the root system is removed during the digging process and that which remains is cut and damaged. Container-grown ornamentals usually have a complete root system, but under- or over-watering while in the container will cause some root death. In addition, container grown plants may have circling roots, which must be pruned at planting time.

Transplanted woody ornamentals typically take three years or more to recover from these traumas and to adapt to new soil and nutrient and moisture conditions. During this time, there is reduced transport of water and nutrients throughout the tree or shrub, making it weak and more susceptible to pathogens and insect borers. Plate 109 shows damage from linden borer larvae (*Saperda vestita*) to a tree that was planted too deeply. In a healthy tree with a strong sap flow, borer eggs that are laid in an existing wound or niche made by the adult borer are likely to be washed away by sap bleeding out of the wound. The borer larvae that hatch and start to tunnel in the tree are likely to drown or to be crushed by the high internal pressures typical in a healthy tree with a strong sap flow.

Canker diseases such as those caused by *Botryosphaeria* and *Cytospora* species occur only on weak or stressed trees. Because the causal fungi are ubiquitous but do not invade healthy trees, they are known as *stress pathogens*. Disease organisms attacking a healthy tree may be walled off and compartmentalized by a tree or shrub by a strong sap flow.

Watering and mulching

The faster an ornamental plant grows new roots, adapts to a site, and returns to a healthy state, the less likely it is to develop disease and insect borer problems. Watering heavily and infrequently provides moisture that the recovering root system needs. Allow the soil to dry out between watering to the point where the newly transplanted tree or shrub is starting to show early signs of wilting. Then water it thoroughly so that the entire root ball becomes moist. Watering too frequently reduces oxygen supply to the roots, causing them to die. Furthermore, turfgrass that is lightly watered frequently tends to produce a shallow root system that is more likely to become stressed during drought, making it more susceptible to patch and other diseases.

Mulching helps to maintain the surface soil moisture between watering, and keeps the shallow roots of newly transplants from drying out and dying. Mulch also helps to keep the soil cool, reducing heat stress on the root system of an ornamental plant transplanted to an exposed location.

The mulched area should extend at least as far as the young transplant's roots, as with the tree shown in plate 110. This not only protects the new root system, but it also eliminates turf and other plants that will compete for nutrients and water. Preventing other plants from growing next to the tree also eliminates injury from line trimmers and lawnmowers. These machines can injure the bark, thereby interrupting the flow of sap. Composted, shredded bark and other organic mulches are preferable. The mulch should be no more than 2 to 3 inches thick, as thick mulch can reduce the flow of oxygen to the root system. In addition, mulch placed against the trunk reduces oxygen exchange at the tree collar, which can kill the tree or shrub. The mulch should be no closer than about 3 inches from the trunk.

Protecting against winter freezing and thawing

Newly planted trees, particularly deciduous trees, are susceptible to frost cracking. During the winter in northern climates, the sap within the trunk will freeze during cold periods. On sunny days, the south and west sides of the trunk may thaw, while the rest of the trunk remains frozen. As a result, the thawed bark will crack or separate from the trunk. This in turn causes death in the cambium area, resulting in reduced flow of sap up and down the trunk, and increasing the likelihood of borer attack and wood rot.

To retard winter thawing, trees have thicker bark on the south and west sides. In addition, lower branches on the tree shade the trunk. Unfortunately, when a tree is transplanted its original orientation is unknown, and as a result, less protected sides are frequently exposed to the winter sun. Furthermore, the lower branches are commonly pruned off at planting time, increasing sun exposure. Even established plants may be damaged by frost cracking if the trunk receives more sun exposure due to the removal of nearby trees, shrubs, or buildings. Because the winter sun is lower in the sky, even the removal of plants or buildings across the street may suddenly increase sun exposure to tree trunks.

To protect exposed trunks, consider using fencing or burlap screens. (Note that the fence does not have to be solid to effectively shade the trunk.) Or, plant evergreen and deciduous shrubs to shade the trunk.

Plant selection and placement

The proper plant in the proper place is a long-held and important axiom of gardening and landscaping. When selecting plants for a landscape or garden, consider hardiness, mature size, light needs, and soil factors (such as moisture,

An old but effective method of protection

Consider this older method of protection for exposed trunks: Paint the trunk with white latex paint diluted with water to a 10-percent mixture (one part paint to nine parts water). The white paint reflects sunlight, reducing heat buildup in the bark. Consisting of only 10 percent paint, the mixture will weather away gradually over two to three years, allowing the bark to thicken gradually during that time. One application before the first winter is all that is needed. Most people apply the paint to all sides of the trunk for appearance sake, even though it is only needed on the south and west sides.

pH, and fertility) as well as appearance. A plant that is properly selected and sited will be healthier, and thus less susceptible to diseases, insect pests, and weeds.

Plant hardiness

Problems with hardiness may be due to either cold or hot temperatures. The range of USDA cold hardiness zones is known for most perennial landscape plants. Whenever a range of hardiness zones is given for a plant, avoid installing plants in a zone outside the recommended range. Plants that are being grown at their cold hardiness limits are more likely to be injured by winter sun exposure and thaws than by cold temperatures. Therefore, these plants will do best on the northeast side of buildings, fences, or tall plantings where they can avoid winter sun exposure and large temperature fluctuations. Plants with marginal cold hardiness may not die outright, but they are more likely to experience dieback from stem cankers because cold-injured tissues allow these opportunistic fungi to invade.

Plants are also susceptible to excessive heat during the summer. For example, pagoda dogwood (*Cornus alternifolia*) commonly dies from cryptodiaporthe canker (*Cryptodiaporthe corni*) when exposed to hot, dry weather. Again, avoid installing plants in zones warmer than those recommended for them. And to increase the likelihood of survival in marginal zones, protect plants from summer sun exposure.

Marginally hardy plants have a better chance of survival in warm areas if the night temperatures are cooler, so plantings near south and west exposures of dark walls are best avoided. If the plant is shade tolerant, it will stay cooler when shaded by trees or buildings. To avoid summer sun exposure when planting on the north or east side of trees and buildings, remember that the sun is higher in the sky in the summer than in the winter, particularly in more northern areas. Therefore, plants need to be located closer to sun-blocking structures for summer sun protection than they do for winter sun protection.

Although a marginally hardy plant may survive temperature extremes, it may be weakened enough to succumb to pest attack. For example, dwarf Alberta spruces (*Picea glauca* 'Conica') planted in zone 6 frequently sustain heavy damage and may die from spider mite infestation. In colder hardiness zones, these trees are rarely damaged by spider mites. Perhaps these cold-adapted plants are less tolerant of spider mite attack in marginal hardiness zones. Winter injury on poplars (*Populus*) predisposes them to cankers, decline, and death. This is common in trees exposed to severe Midwest winters but uncommon in the Pacific Northwest where winters are mild.

Sun versus shade

Many shade-tolerant plants grow well or actually better in full sun, but the opposite is not true. Trees, shrubs, flowers, and other plants that are not shade-adapted are small and spindly when grown in shade and are more susceptible to diseases and insect pests. Mosses are common weeds in shady areas, particularly where there is high soil moisture.

Mature plant size

When designing a landscape, always consider the mature size of the plants you select. A common mistake is to plant trees and shrubs too close together. Although it is easy to overplant when the plants are small, to avoid leaving large gaps in the landscape, the resulting mature landscape is too shady for the survival of turf or even most ground covers. Shrubs frequently grow together to form a shapeless mass if not aggressively pruned. A common approach is to overplant initially and then remove some of the plants as the landscape matures. But because it is particularly difficult psychologically to remove healthy plants, it is preferable to accept a sparse landscape while the

Selecting turfgrasses

For lawns in shady locations, select fine fescues, (*Festuca*) and other shade-tolerant turfgrasses. Tall fescue (*F. elatior*), Kentucky bluegrass (*Poa pratensis*), *Zoysia*, and other turfgrasses that do well in full sun are unlikely to thrive in shady areas, leaving areas of bare soil for weeds to colonize.

Plant a seed mix or select sod with a mixture of species and varieties. Some grass species will sprout more quickly, providing cover and reducing weed invasion. The mixture of species and varieties improves the likelihood that there will be reduced susceptibility among some of them to diseases.

Planting near buildings and in small spaces

Knowing the mature size of plants is important when planting near a building or in a small space. Trees and shrubs that grow too large for the site will rub against buildings or crowd other plants. Not only are they likely to damage the siding and the roof, but the rubbing is likely to create wounds that will allow bacteria, fungi, and wood-boring insects to enter plants. Although pruning can help control the size of a large plant, severe pruning is likely to result in an unhealthy, less attractive plant that is more susceptible to diseases than plants allowed to grow naturally.

plants are young and small. Another approach is to plant larger, older specimens, but these are more expensive and usually take longer to adapt to a site than smaller, younger plants.

Soil fertility and pH

A soil pH of between 6.2 and 6.8 is ideal for most plants. A pH of 7 is neutral, so most plants prefer soils that are slightly acidic. In the northeastern United States, soils tend to be more acidic; in the western United States, soils

Soil pH across the United States

In the northeastern United States, where soils tend to be more acidic, it is best to avoid certain western species of pine, spruce, and juniper that are adapted to alkaline soils. In western and some midwestern U.S. locations, avoid plants that require acidic soils, such as blueberry (*Vaccinium*), azalea and rhododendron, holly (*Ilex*), pin oak, paper birch (*Betula papyrifera*) and red maple. In the Midwest, both higher pH soils and poor drainage contribute to phytophthora root rot, with subsequent decline or death of rhododendrons.

tend to be alkaline (above 7 pH). Many plants tolerate a range of soil pH, but plants in soils that are too acidic or too alkaline tend to develop chlorotic leaves (as shown in plate 111), experience dieback, and be generally unhealthy and susceptible to pests.

A soil test will determine the pH. For vegetables and annual flowers, it is easy to adjust the soil pH annually or biennially using lime to increase the pH, or aluminum sulphate or sulphur to reduce it. For perennial flowers, shrubs, and trees, it is more difficult to adjust soil pH. Although soil pH can be adjusted at planting time, the buffering capacity of the soil will counteract any adjustments made within a few years.

Applying fertilizer

Fertility is easier to adjust than soil pH is. Some soil pH tests also provide fertility information. A variety of fertilizers, both mineral and organic, are available. Mineral fertilizers are typically mined from the earth or produced through chemical synthesis or purification. They tend to be higher in concentration than organic fertilizers. Organic fertilizers are derived from recently living plants or animals and include mulches, leaf mold, cottonseed meal, blood meal, and bone meal. Many scientists have determined that a plant will utilize nutrients equally whether the source is mineral or organic; however, many gardeners feel that organic fertilized vegetables taste better.

The concentration of the macronutrients nitrogen, phosphorus, and potassium are given as numbers on a fertilizer label in that order. For exam-

A caution about overfertilization

Overfertilization can increase susceptibility to some insects. Sap-feeding insects—such as aphids, whiteflies, soft scales, and spider mites—experience much higher levels of growth and reproduction on plants growing in nitrogen-rich soil. However, nitrogen fertilization reduces the growth rate of some tree-feeding caterpillars and other insects. Excess nitrogen produced by overfertilization causes lush growth in the spring, which is most susceptible to fire blight.

ple, fertilizer listed as 12-10-13 contains 12 percent nitrogen, 10 percent phosphorus, and 13 percent potassium.

Recommendations for applying fertilizer are commonly given in pounds, usually nitrogen, per acre or thousand square feet. For example, to apply 2 pounds of nitrogen per thousand square feet, one would need to apply 20 pounds of a 10-8-8 fertilizer or 100 pounds of a 2-1-1 fertilizer. *Be aware of the nutrient analysis of the fertilizers you apply, read and follow the labels carefully, and use them to adjust* known *soil deficiencies.* Never apply fertilizer until you have tested the soil to determine whether it is warranted.

Trees and shrubs generally require little or no fertilization, but avoid planting them in soils with poor fertility, to reduce nutrient-deficiency diseases such as chlorosis and stunting. Flowers and vegetables grown in low-fertility soils will be stunted and have small flowers and fruit. Their leaves may be yellowish or otherwise off-color. White clover (*Trifolium repens*) is prevalent in turf areas with low fertility. This nitrogen-fixing plant may actually increase the fertility of the soil for other plants.

Crop rotation

Many diseases of vegetables and flowers are soil borne because many pathogenic fungi and nematodes live in the soil. Pathogenic fungi can exist for a long period of time *saprophytically,* living on decaying plant material in the soil. Clubroot of cabbage (*Plasmodiophora brassicae*) and other cole crops, fusarium wilt, and verticillium wilt are examples of fungal diseases that can exist in the soil for extended time periods.

Rotating closely related vegetables to different areas of the garden on a yearly basis avoids some diseases that can greatly reduce the yield or even the survivability of many garden crops (figure 16). Table 2 lists common related vegetable plant groups that should not be planted in the same soil year after year.

Crop rotation can also help to reduce insect pests. In field crops, rotating the location of corn is very effective in reducing root feeding by corn rootworm larvae. Damage by this insect is rarely a problem in home gardens, but feeding on the green corn silks by the adult beetles can be serious. Annually rotating sweet corn in the garden should reduce the number of corn rootworm adults. In some areas, rootworms may be a problem even in rotated corn. In portions of Illinois and Indiana, western corn rootworms lay eggs in the soil of crops other than corn. As a result, larval damage is prevalent in corn planted in that soil the next year.

Figure 16. Vegetable garden designed for efficient crop rotation. Photo courtesy of Philip L. Nixon

Table 2. Related vegetables that should be rotated annually to other garden locations

Cole crops	Solanaceous crops	Cucurbit crops
broccoli	eggplant	cantaloupe
brussels sprouts	flowering tobacco	cucumber
cabbage	pepper	gourd
collards	potato	watermelon
kale	tomato	squash

Squash bug is very specific to feeding on squash. Adults overwinter in and near the garden under debris and emerge the following spring. If a garden is isolated from other gardens, a two-year rotation of planting squash will greatly reduce infestations. Biennial squash planting causes adult squash bugs to fly a long distance to infest the crop. Typically, few bugs find the crop, and these tend to arrive later in the season—producing fewer nymphs and less subsequent damage.

Timing planting and harvest

Try always to plant during the best growing conditions for successful establishment of the species you are planting. For example, it is best to plant trees and shrubs in the spring or fall, when it easier for them to survive with the increased rainfall, moderate temperatures, and cloudy days associated with these seasons. Similarly, spring planting of vegetables and flowers provides for a longer growing season.

Planting at the proper time can also help to avoid some pest problems, as these examples show:

- Corn earworm is unable to overwinter consistently in the northern half of the United States; therefore, sweet corn that is planted early enough to be harvested in July usually remains free of this pest.

- Bean leaf beetle feeds as an adult on bean pods, and this pest becomes more numerous throughout the season. Garden beans that are planted earlier and therefore harvested earlier have less pod damage than those planted later in the season.

- In areas where soybeans are commonly planted, however, it is important to plant garden beans no earlier than farmers plant their soybeans because overwintering bean leaf beetle adults will concentrate on and destroy garden beans emerging before the soybeans.

- Potato leafhopper (*Empoasca fabae*) damage, shown in plate 112, can impact the size of a potato harvest. As the growing season progresses, potato leafhoppers become more numerous. Potatoes planted and harvested earlier will bear more potatoes than those planted later.

- Grasshoppers are larger and eat more as the growing season progresses, causing heavy damage to a wide array of vegetables and flowers. Planting early results in larger plants that are less likely to be heavily damaged.

- Squash vine borer adults fly and lay eggs from late spring into early summer, selecting larger plants or plants that have started to vine. Squash planted in early summer will escape egg-laying and still produce a crop before frost.

- Late-planted squash plants are smaller and more susceptible to squash bug injury. Squash bug adults are long lived and continue to lay eggs throughout the growing season.

Irrigation and watering

Turf

With lawns, the timing of irrigation or watering is important for managing white grubs. During early summer, adult Japanese beetle, masked chafers (*Cyclocephala*), and other white grubs dig into the soil to lay eggs. Apparently these insects are attracted to green, actively growing lawns. It is common in the midwestern and northeastern United States for unwatered cool-season turfgrasses to become dormant, dry, and brown, due to high temperatures and infrequent rainfall at this time of year. Adult beetles prefer irrigated lawns for egg-laying—probably because dry soil is difficult to dig into, high soil temperatures cause egg mortality, and brown grass is a poor food for larvae. Therefore, it is best to avoid irrigating in early summer if possible. Rest assured that late-season late summer and early fall rainfall or irrigation accompanied by cooler temperatures will allow the turf to resprout from rhizomes and crowns and grow into a lush, green lawn.

In late summer into fall, white grubs typically cause the greatest amount of turfgrass damage by feeding on the roots (such as the damage from masked chafer bugs shown in plate 98). Irrigated turf grows faster than unwatered turf, so if there is a moderately damaging white grub population, then irrigating the turf at this time of year will help it to tolerate the grub feeding. Remember to irrigate infrequently but heavily and early enough in the day for the grass blades to dry by nightfall. Leaves that are wet for long time periods are more susceptible to fungus attack. Furthermore, as mentioned earlier, turfgrasses that are watered frequently and lightly are more susceptible to patch diseases when exposed to hot temperatures or drought.

As winter approaches, the grubs descend deeper into the soil to escape cold temperatures. In the spring, they ascend to resume feeding on the roots. However, spring rains and cool temperatures cause cool-season grasses to grow roots faster than the grubs can eat them, allowing the grass to tolerate an infestation.

Other plants

Trees, shrubs, flowers, and vegetables growing in constantly moist soils are susceptible to root rots. Excess water eliminates air spaces in the soil, causing roots to be injured from lack of oxygen. These damaged roots are susceptible to water mold pathogens such as *Pythium* and *Phytophthora*, causing the death of seedlings as well as older plants.

Frequent, light watering is not advised, as it tends to promote shallow root systems. Plants with shallow root systems are more likely to be moisture stressed during a drought and less capable of tolerating pests. It is therefore preferable to provide heavy, less frequent irrigation, particularly during dry periods—to promote roots that grow deep into the soil where moisture is more consistent.

Aerification

Lawn and garden soils frequently have a disturbed soil profile. During house construction, subsoil from basement excavation is spread over the soil around the house, and this soil becomes compacted by heavy equipment. Once the house is completed, a few inches of topsoil are applied over this compacted subsoil. If the soil is not rototilled, cultivated, or mixed in some other manner, an interface comes into being between the two different soils. This interface results in shallowly rooted landscape and garden plants that do not penetrate the underlying, compacted subsoil very effectively. If muck-based sod is laid on top of this soil, a second interface arises between the muck and the mineral soil. Thus, properly seeding a new lawn or laying down mineral-based sod usually results in a healthier lawn.

Aerification, which is a method of disturbing soil so that air more efficiently penetrates the soil, is useful in breaking up these interfaces in a lawn that is already in place. Here is how it works:

1. A core-aerifying machine punches many closely spaced holes into the soil and removes plugs that are several inches long.
2. The plugs are allowed to remain on the surface, where they dry and break up.
3. The resulting holes, approximately 1/2 inch in diameter, provide open area for roots to grow into the next layer.
4. After several years of annual aerification, the interfaces are eliminated, resulting in deeper rooted, healthier plants less susceptible to diseases and insect pests.

An aerified lawn also helps to eliminate a thick thatch layer, making it easier for grass roots to penetrate deeper into the soil—and making the lawn less susceptible to turfgrass patch diseases and chinch bugs (*Blissus*).

Aerification is also useful in loosening compacted soil in footpaths, along sidewalks, and in other locations. These are typically bare soil areas or areas that have weeds such as knotweed (*Polygonum*), carpetweed (*Mollugo*, shown in plate 113), and sandburs (*Cenchrus*) that will tolerate compacted soils. Hoeing, spading, or rototilling will loosen the soil several inches deep, allowing desirable plants to thrive in these areas.

Chinch bugs in turfgrass

Chinch bugs are more common in lawns with a thick, dry, thatch layer. Naturally occurring insect-attacking fungi usually keep chinch bugs under control. In lawns with little or no thatch, the chinch bugs live close to the moist soil where the fungi are numerous and will attack the bugs.

Chapter 6

Physical Pest Management

The methods for physically removing a pest from a plant or preventing the pest from reaching the plant are known as physical or mechanical pest management. Management practices include weed-pulling, cultivating, pruning out disease and insect infestations, and using screens and other barriers to keep pests from reaching protected plants. Probably the oldest pest control methods are mechanical. Pest management may have started with our prehistoric ancestors, removing lice and their eggs from one another's scalps and driving off competing animals from a kill with a club.

Directly removing pests by handpicking is probably the surest method of pest control. When you physically remove a pest, you know that you have forever eliminated that individual from your landscape or garden. When one considers nonchemical control methods, this one is almost always available for weeds and insect pests. The main drawback to this method is that it is time-consuming and labor intensive.

Theoretically, creating and maintaining a home garden or landscape is not considered a for-profit activity, and many of us consider it a leisure activity—and as such, time-consuming activities should not be a problem. Physical pest management activities can even be considered stress relieving. After a hard day at work, we can relieve pent-up frustrations by squishing bugs and pulling weeds out of the ground. These and other activities are physical pest control.

Removing weeds

Pulling weeds is probably the most obvious and most common method of physical pest management. Indeed, grasping the weed low on the stem and pulling it out by the roots may be the most common garden activity. Large weeds, particularly weedy grasses, have large root systems that may be difficult to pull up without breaking off the stem, leaving the root system wholly or mostly intact. Grasses in particular tend to grow back if the root system is left behind. Furthermore, the removal of large weeds may dislodge adjacent garden plants or loosen their roots enough to harm flowers and vegetables.

Fortunately, weeding knives, weed hooks, short-handled hoes, trowels, and other tools are available for loosening the root systems of large weeds, making them easier to pull and less likely to disturb the roots of garden plants. One technique effective in reducing disturbance to the garden plant's root system is to hold down the soil next to a garden plant with one hand while pulling an adjacent weed with the other hand. Pulling seedlings and younger weeds is typically much less disturbing to garden plants.

Hoeing

With row-planted vegetables and flowers, it is easy and more efficient to eliminate the weeds by hoeing between rows and alongside rows. Most

Identifying weed seedlings

A concern with early weeding is identification. Weeds are much more difficult to identify as seedlings than when they are older. It can be challenging to tell which plants are weeds, and which are vegetables or flowers. Identification guides for weed seedlings are much less common than guides for mature weeds. An option is to identify the seedling vegetables and flowers and pull everything else. If the crop has been planted in rows, then the weeds are easier to detect. Some seed packets have illustrations of the seedling vegetable or flower, making seedling-weed determination easier. Pull all weeds you can identify as soon as possible, but when in doubt, leave the plant until later when identification is easier.

Figure 17. Hoeing deeply removes the weed's root system and cultivates the soil. Photo courtesy of Philip L. Nixon

weeds, particularly weed seedlings can be killed merely by cutting off the aboveground portions by sliding the hoe along the ground. Hoeing deeper into the ground (as shown in figure 17) has the advantage of removing the weeds' root systems and also cultivates the soil, which can improve aeration and water penetration. It also disturbs the root system of emerging weed seedlings, killing them or seriously inhibiting their growth.

Hoes, shovels, and other tools have cutting edges that allow them to cut off weeds or enter the soil more easily. For efficient weeding, keep the blades of these tools sharp by sharpening at least twice daily, or carrying a file to sharpen the tool as needed throughout the day. When sharpening the tool, follow the bevel that is already present on the cutting edge. How sharp to keep it honed depends on personal preference, but remember: *Always exercise caution when using garden tools*. A sharpened tool may be more likely to cut human flesh than a dull one. However, a dull hoe is more likely to skip off the hard soil surface and cause injury. A sharpened hoe or shovel will make weeding or digging much easier.

Cultivating

More efficient for weed removal than either hand pulling or hoeing is cultivation. All of the various push cultivators, garden tractor attachments, and garden tillers have shovels or tines that push through or cut through the soil, disturbing the root system of weeds and turning over the soil. Even large weeds are easily dislodged and killed or seriously damaged by these tools. Cultivation can effectively eliminate most of the weeds in the garden very quickly.

There are some concerns with cultivation, however:

- Cultivation brings weed seeds that were deep in the soil closer to the surface where they can germinate. After cultivation, as many new weeds may sprout as were killed through cultivation.
- Because during cultivation moist underlying soil is brought to the surface, moisture may be more easily lost to evaporation. During droughts and in dry climates, this can be a major concern.
- Cultivation becomes limited as vegetables and flowers grow larger because the cultivator is more likely to bruise and break stems, leaves, and flowers. Cultivation is also likely to disturb root systems of larger vegetables and flowers as the roots grow between the rows to locate additional moisture and nutrients.
- Avoid cultivating when the soil is wet. Dislodged weeds are more likely to take root and survive in wet soil; whereas, on dry soil, exposed roots wither. In addition, working wet soil causes it to set and turn hard, making it difficult for seedling emergence and root growth.
- Be sure to cultivate just before planting. This synchronizes new weed germination with garden seed sprouting, giving garden plants a better chance of competing with the weeds.

Hand pulling

The best way to pull weeds in beds of ground covers, perennial flowers, and other small areas is by hand. Weed beds of ground covers such as common periwinkle (*Vinca minor*) wintercreeper euonymus, pachysandra, hosta, and barren strawberry (*Waldsteinia ternata*) on a frequent basis by walking through the bed and pulling weeds that stick up above the ground cover. Pulling weeds is also easy around the root bases of trees and along fences and foundations. Large lawn areas are less effectively weeded by hand, but by doing so, you can avoid using herbicides.

Hand tools for weeding are available. Dandelion diggers, for example, have a forked, sharp head that cuts off the dandelion taproot below the soil surface. When the taproot is severed, it will grow back new leaves and stems, but the plant will be smaller than before. Repeated removal throughout the growing season will be needed to reduce the dandelion population in a lawn seriously.

Mechanical pulling and trimming

Mechanical weed pullers, dandelion diggers, and weed knives are effective in eliminating individual weeds, particularly those with root systems less extensive than those of dandelions. Hand grass shears, grass sickles, hand pruners, and other hand tools all effectively cut off the aboveground portion of weeds, resulting in the death of the root system in many species.

Hand-held and push line trimmers easily and quickly remove the weed portions growing above ground covers. In the case of taller ground covers, such as hosta, pachysandra, and ferns, this leaves behind enough of the lower stem and leaves of the weeds to allow the weed to regrow. However, consistent trimming will keep the bed looking neat, and the weeds will be unlikely to receive sufficient light to flower and seed below the ground-cover canopy. Line trimmers are also effective along building foundations, raised bed timbers, and fences. Avoid using them around trees, particularly younger trees and shrubs, because the line will cut through the bark into the cambium, resulting in decline and possible death. Careless use of a lawnmower can cause similar injury, as shown in figure 18.

Mowing

Pigweed (*Amaranthus retroflexus*), lamb's quarters (*Chenopodium album*), and many other weed species are absent from lawns because they cannot tolerate mowing. However, many weeds tolerate mowing; otherwise, there would be no lawn weeds.

Mowing is also an option for controlling weed growth in sidewalk cracks, along the edges of parking areas, and in noncrop garden areas. If you consis-

Figure 18. Tree with a large burl and bark damage due to lawnmower injury. Photo courtesy of Philip L. Nixon

tently mow sidewalk cracks and other small areas, then turfgrasses from adjoining areas will be able to infiltrate, resulting in a more attractive appearance over time. Likewise, by consistently mowing a small bare area, such as an old garden space, you can enable turfgrasses to creep in eventually—thus saving you the labor and expense of seeding or sodding.

The weed that doubles as a ground cover

The weed creeping Charlie or ground ivy (*Glechoma hederacea*) is also a ground cover. Able to grow in almost total shade, it tolerates damp soils and mowing and thrives on neglect. It provides an excellent ground cover in heavily shaded areas that would otherwise be bare. Scattered weeds growing above the ground ivy are easy to control and keep short with mowing. Mowing makes the ground ivy denser and more attractive.

Removing diseases

It is more difficult to manage diseases physically. Although it is easy to remove the fruiting bodies and spore masses that fungi produce, the main part of the disease organism consists of fungal hyphae that are usually present within much of the plant. For example, wood rot fungi produce conks (mushroom fruiting bodies; shown in plate 114) on the side of tree trunks, but removing them does nothing to eliminate the fungal hyphae in the wood that are causing the wood to rot. Root rots typically produce mushrooms in fairy rings and other patterns that are easy to remove. Once again, however, the hyphae that produce these fruiting structures are not disturbed.

Removing diseased leaves

By picking off and disposing affected leaves, you can reduce leaf spot, botrytis, and other localized diseases. This method removes not only the unsightly leaves from the plant, but also a source of inoculum that can infect the same plant or other plants. Avoid dropping the leaves under the plants, because many diseases will continue to produce spores on the discarded leaves, and these can splash up onto plants during rainfall and irrigation. Similarly, removing diseased leaves and twigs that have dropped off the plant eliminates a source of fungal spores.

Pruning

It is probably easier to transmit diseases physically than it is to remove them physically. When pruning plants, always clean and disinfect tools each time you move to a new plant. This is very important when pruning to remove diseased material. When pruning trees with fire blight, clean and disinfect tools after each cut, following these steps:

1. Clean off deposits of sap, bark, sawdust, and other plant material.
2. Wash or wipe the tools with isopropyl alcohol (rubbing alcohol) or a 10-percent bleach solution to eliminate most of the plant pathogens on them.

Pruning to control fire blight

Pruning is commonly recommended for removing fire blight from plants. However, this bacterial infection typically spreads far beyond the branch tip that is curled and blackened. Prune affected stems well below the damaged area, at least 8 to 10 inches below any symptoms. Typically, remove as much of the branch as possible without destroying the aesthetic quality of the tree or shrub. In the spring, be watchful for bark areas oozing sap, shown in plate 115—and prune these out immediately, as bees and other insects tend to be attracted to these areas to feed. When visiting other plants, the bees and other insects can spread the fire blight bacteria.

An easy way to do this is to carry a few individually packaged alcohol swabs, available at most pharmacies. Use a fresh swab to disinfect the tool before moving to the next plant.

Removing the entire plant

At times, the best IPM method to protect other plants from infestation is to remove the entire infested plant. Aphids and leafhoppers transmit viruses and phytoplasmas between plants. These sucking insects can be numerous, and only one is needed to infect a plant. Because eliminating these insects is very difficult, it is usually more effective to eliminate infected plants as they become noticeable. Aster yellows is a phytoplasma, carried by a leafhopper, that commonly kills marigold, nasturtium, and other flowers. One management method is to replace entire beds with new transplants, which will stay attractive for the rest of the growing season.

Dutch elm disease and oak wilt are fungal diseases spread both by insects and root grafts between plants. Quickly removing infested trees is effective in reducing the spread and incidence of these diseases. If susceptible trees are growing close enough to spread the disease through root grafts, it is best to remove not only the diseased tree but also the healthy ones next to it. By the time a tree shows disease symptoms, the fungus has likely spread to other trees.

Some tree species dying of oak wilt form mycelial mats, or pressure pads, under the bark. Sap beetles feed on these mats and carry spores to other trees when they feed at open wounds. Because this occurs primarily during spring and early summer, be sure to remove dead limbs or infested trees by late winter. During spring and early summer, avoid pruning healthy trees to prevent sap beetles from transmitting fungi to pruning wounds.

Removing beetles

It is easy to remove insects by hand as long as they are large enough to be grasped and move slowly enough to be captured. Adult Japanese beetles, weevils, and many other beetles react to disturbance by folding their legs and dropping to the ground. Most beetles remain motionless for a few seconds, but adult weevils remain motionless for an extended period. Many adult weevils are dark in color, which allows them to blend into the soil and makes them very difficult to see. Birds, lizards, and other predators tend to be attracted to prey that moves, so dropping and remaining motionless is probably a good survival tactic.

This behavior can make handpicking easier. One method is to hold a container with rubbing alcohol or soapy water underneath the insect with one hand while disturbing the insect with the other hand. When the beetle drops into the container, it will be killed by the alcohol or drown in the soapy water. Soap or detergent reduces the water surface tension so that insects are unable to float or swim.

Other than Japanese beetles, various adult beetles can be controlled by handpicking, but seldom are they serious enough pests to warrant the labor. Young and recently transplanted trees are most likely to be harmed by heavy leaf feeding damage; older, established trees are less likely to be seriously harmed. Thus, trees that stand to benefit most from insect control are small enough that insect hand-removal is easily accomplished from the ground or a small ladder.

Adult strawberry root weevil (*Otiorhynchus ovatus*), black vine weevil (*O. sulcatus*), and imported longhorned weevil (*Calomycterus setarius*) do most of their feeding at night. Strawberry root weevil adults eat the edges of the flower petals of black-eyed Susans, chrysanthemums, daisies, and roses—as shown in plate 117. Although they also feed on the leaves in a similar man-

Controlling Japanese beetles

Japanese beetle adults, shown in plate 116, are sun-loving insects—found primarily on the upper, sunniest leaves of the plant and typically upper side of the leaf. This makes it very easy to locate and handpick the beetles on small trees, shrubs, and garden plants.

When Japanese beetles feed on leaves, the leaves produce a chemical that attracts more beetles. Therefore, handpicking Japanese beetle adults daily or every other day for the first couple of weeks after they emerge in early summer can reduce the number of beetles and associated damage throughout the season.

Adult Japanese beetles tend to change host plants every three days, and when they fly to a new host, they typically travel 0.75 to 1.5 miles. This takes them out of a landscape and into other areas. Because of this frequent and long dispersal pattern, controlling beetles in a landscape has little effect on the number of eggs laid and turf-damaging grubs later in the season. Control adult Japanese beetles to reduce adult feeding damage, not subsequent lawn damage by the larvae.

ner, the damage is usually heaviest on flowers. Black vine weevil adults eat notches out of the leaf edges of strawberry, wintercreeper euonymus, yew (*Taxus*), azalea, rhododendron, clematis, and various other plants. Imported longhorned weevil adults feed on the leaves of a wide range of trees and shrubs.

Because all three of these pests feed primarily at night, hand-removal must be done at night. Many night-feeding insects do not appear to be affected by artificial light, except usually to stop feeding when illuminated. Nonetheless, because insects typically cannot see the red section of the light spectrum, using a red bulb or red lens on a flashlight will help to ensure that the insects do not flee.

Conifer-feeding weevils are also nocturnal and easily removed by hand. Adult northern pine weevil (*Pissodes nemorensis*), pales weevil (*Hylobius pales*), and pine root collar weevil (*H. radicis*) hide during the day in debris beneath the tree. At night, the adult weevils climb the tree to feed on the bark of young shoots and twigs, causing dieback and brown needles. As with other adult beetles, these insects fold their legs and drop when disturbed.

Bark beetle larvae feed in the cambium of dead and dying trees, and adults are strongly attracted to these trees for egg laying. When a pine or other conifer is dying, the adult bark beetles attack not only the dying tree, but also nearby trees in large numbers. This heavy beetle attack can cause healthy trees to decline, attracting more beetles. These trees die, and healthy trees next to them are attacked and eventually killed. Over several years, an entire row of conifers planted as a windbreak or screen can be devastated. To prevent this, promptly remove dead or dying conifers close to others of the same species.

Removing caterpillars

Also controlled by handpicking are caterpillars, although they are usually harder to remove from the plant than beetles are. The claws at the ends of the caterpillar's true legs grasp tightly, as do the hooks at the ends of the prolegs. Like beetles, collected caterpillars can be dropped into containers of rubbing alcohol or soapy water.

Tomato hornworms are probably the easiest to remove by hand. These caterpillars attack tomato and other solanaceous crops such as pepper, potato, eggplant, and flowering tobacco. When reaching maturity, a single caterpillar can eat the entire top out of a large, mature tomato plant overnight. The caterpillars feed primarily at night—during the day hiding on or under leaves deeper into the plant, where their green color makes them difficult to see. Early in the morning, you will find caterpillars at the top of plants, where you can easily see and remove them.

Cabbageworms are also susceptible to handpicking. Imported cabbageworms (*Pieris rapae*) and cabbage loopers (*Trichoplusia ni*) are slow-moving caterpillars that are easily found on the undersides of leaves and at the base of cabbage heads. However, the larvae of the diamondback moth (*Plutella xylostella*) are small caterpillars that wiggle violently when disturbed, making them very difficult to catch.

Bagworms live in spindle-shaped bags that can be effectively handpicked from their hosts, as shown in plate 118. They tend to feed at the top of the tree and work their way down, making a ladder necessary to reach most of the population even on smaller trees. The eggs overwinter in the bags of the females; therefore, handpicking from fall through late spring is particularly effective. Do not drop the overwintering bags under the tree because the hatching larvae will climb the tree.

Caterpillars such as fall webworm, eastern tent caterpillar, and yellow-necked caterpillar are considered *gregarious*, or colonial: They typically feed in large numbers, causing feeding damage to be very noticeable, even when large trees are attacked. Several of these insects live in silk tents, making them easy to find, remove, and eliminate. Fall webworms construct large silk tents over the ends of branches while they feed on the leaves inside the tent. Prune or pull these tents off the tree with the caterpillars inside.

Eastern tent caterpillar also constructs a silk tent, but in a branch crotch where the larvae stay at night and on cloudy days. During the day, the caterpillars move out onto the foliage to feed. Remove the silk tent at night or on a cloudy or rainy day. By early summer, these caterpillars lay 0.5-inch-long egg masses that surround large twigs and remain on the tree throughout the summer, fall, and winter. Plate 119 shows an eastern tent caterpillar egg mass. It is easier to handpick or prune off the reddish-brown egg masses during the winter because they are more visible when the trees are leafless. Dispose of the egg masses, as any dropped under the tree can hatch into caterpillars that will then climb the tree.

Yellownecked caterpillars (*Datana ministra*) and walnut caterpillars (*D. integerrima*) are gregarious, feeding in groups on many tree species. They defoliate one branch before moving to another, and the defoliated branches make it easier to locate the pest. Remove masses of these caterpillars by pruning off an infested branch or by pulling them off the branch by hand.

Gypsy moths commonly lay their eggs on the trunk or at the base of trees in midsummer. They lay many eggs in the open, but some under loose bark and on fallen leaves and other debris. You can scrape off egg masses with a spatula or knife and put them into rubbing alcohol or soapy water. Or, you can treat them with an insecticidal spray oil and leave them on the tree. It is possible to control whitemarked tussock moth (*Orgyia leucostigma*) in a similar manner.

Removing other insects, mites, and mollusks

Many sawflies, including European pine sawfly (*Neodiprion sertifer*), redheaded pine sawfly (*N. lecontei*), white pine sawfly (*N. pinetum*), and dusky birch sawfly (*Croesus latitarsus*), have gregarious larvae. When disturbed, the larvae will curl their front and posterior ends up into the air in unison, making them easier to see. The brown leaves and defoliated branches that their feeding causes also aids in locating them.

Control scales and mealybugs on trees, shrubs, and houseplants by rubbing off individuals or by pruning out heavily infested areas. Physical removal is useful in reducing the population, making the introduction of natural enemies or other control measures more successful. Scale removal once or twice per year, during each generation, should be sufficient to control scales in temperate climates. Tropical scale and mealybug species complete generations approximately every three months. Weekly inspections of infested plants and removal of pests for three to four months should be effective.

Carpenterworms (*Prionoxystus robiniae*) create large tunnels about 0.5 inches in diameter that ascend relatively straight up the center of the limb or trunk. The caterpillar keeps the hole open by pushing frass out of it, causing it to accumulate below the hole. You can insert a wire into the hole and push upward until it reaches, pierces, and kills the larva. This method is less effective on other caterpillar borers that tend to make smaller, more winding tunnels. It is completely ineffective on beetle borers because they do not maintain open tunnels.

Squash vine borer larvae tunnel upward from the base of squash and related garden plants. This insect hollows out the stem while feeding and keeps the stem hollow by expelling frass. Attacked plants have frass emerging from a hole at the base of the plant. You can:

1. Locate the larvae by pinching gently up the stem starting at the base. Just below where the stem feels solid is where the larvae will be located.
2. Slit the stem open with a knife at that point, and destroy or remove the borer larvae. Be sure to look carefully for multiple larvae, as it is common for there to be as many as twenty larvae per stem.
3. Gently press the stem back together and wrap it with plastic or another nonporous material.

Squash vine borer adult moths lay their eggs at the base of the plant. The pinhead-sized, reddish-brown eggs are laid singly from about 0.5 inches above the ground to 0.5 inches below the ground. Inspecting the plants two or three times per week and removing eggs can greatly reduce the number of borers in the plants. Adult squash vine borer females are red and black, 1-inch-long, wasp-like moths that tend to sit on the upper side of bean and squash leaves in the early morning. At this time of the day, they are slow moving, and you can easily handpick them.

It is possible to collect squash bug adults in large numbers where they overwinter in the debris of their host plants from late fall into early winter. During the summer, adults lay masses of up to approximately thirty reddish-brown eggs on the host plant leaves. Most egg masses will be on the leaf undersides at the base of the major leaf veins, as shown in plate 120. Scouting for these eggs two or three times per week and removing them will reduce the number of bugs attacking the plants.

Slugs and snails are also active at night on garden plants. It is possible to collect large numbers of them in a short time during the night or at dawn, before they retreat to daytime hiding places. Drop them into a container of rubbing alcohol or soapy water.

Aphids, spittlebug nymphs, plant bug nymphs, and pest mites (including mite eggs) can be knocked off plants with forceful sprays of water. A hose with a nozzle is effective on shrubs, vegetables, flowers, and other small plants. A pesticide sprayer containing water only is effective for small trees.

When using this method, adjust the force of the water so that it is strong enough to dislodge the insects but not forceful enough to damage the plants. Ferns and other thin-leaved plants are too fragile for this method to be useful. However, if mite infestations are present, even fragile plants can be misted or lightly sprayed two or three times per day to increase the humidity around the plants, thus increasing the incidence of fungus on the mites and obtaining control.

Trapping insects and mollusks

Trapping devices are generally used to capture large numbers of pests. They rely on the behavior of the pest to be attracted to them for shelter or food.

Place traps where the pest normally travels. During the day, slugs and snails seek out protected areas that are dark and humid. Remove fallen leaves and other debris that make attractive hiding areas, and then lay boards or other flat objects on moist soil. During the day, you are likely to find large numbers of slugs under these objects where they are easy to collect. To increase the effectiveness of traps for slugs and snails, add a food source. Sinking a shallow dish to ground level and adding stale beer, rotting banana peels, or other decaying plant material will attract slugs and snails. Adding a cover over the dish that is supported by pebbles or twigs will increase effectiveness. One advantage of using beer in the trap is that the slugs and snails will be killed, so none will escape the trap.

Squash bug nymphs and adults seek protected areas during the day. Removing fallen leaves and other debris that serve as hiding places will force them to congregate under the boards and other objects that you have placed on the ground. When collecting hiding bugs, look under fruit and leaves laying on the ground for additional bugs.

Earwigs also seek refuge in protected areas, such as cracks and crevices, during the day. Large populations of them can be very damaging to roses, daylilies (*Hemerocallis*), marigolds, zinnias, and other flowers. Foot-long sections of garden hose or rolled up newspapers laid on the soil will attract earwigs during the night. In the morning, pick up these traps, holding one end over a container of rubbing alcohol or soapy water, and then tap with the other hand to cause the earwigs to fall into the container.

Gypsy moth and elm leaf beetle larvae descend host trees to molt and pupate. Trap them using the following technique:

1. Tie a foot-wide strip of burlap or other coarse cloth loosely around the trunk of the host tree, using a piece of twine or rope across the center of the cloth.
2. Drape the upper half of the cloth over the lower half.
3. When larvae descend the tree to molt or to pupate and hide in the folds of the cloth, collect and destroy them.

Elm leaf beetle larvae also pupate at the base of trees, in early and late summer. Place some fallen leaves or straw at the tree's base to provide cover and encourage more larvae to pupate there. Then, remove the leaves or straw to expose the pupae.

Adult apple maggots (*Rhagoletis pomonella*) are attracted to red apples as well as to red spherical traps coated with sticky glue—like the one shown in figure 19. Because the adults emerge several weeks before the apples turn red, place traps in trees early in the season to trap and kill many of these flies, reducing later infestation.

Figure 19. Red sphere trap for apple maggot adults. Photo courtesy of Philip L. Nixon

Yellow sticky traps are used primarily for monitoring populations of winged aphids, whiteflies, thrips, and fungus gnats in greenhouses. They are effective because the adults appear to be attracted to yellow more than they are to the green plants on which they feed. You can use these traps to reduce whitefly numbers on indoor plants. Hang them just above the canopy of infested plants. Then, disturb the foliage at least once or twice daily to cause the adult whiteflies to fly up and be captured by the yellow sticky trap.

Using barriers to control weeds

Organic mulches, newspapers, black plastic sheeting, weed barrier fabric, and various other materials make effective barriers to kill weeds or prevent them from emerging. Organic mulches, such as compost, fallen tree leaves, or grass clippings, must be at least 2 to 3 inches thick and free of weed seeds. Newspapers must be applied several layers thick to prevent weed penetration. The area need not be weed-free when you apply the barrier, because the barrier will keep light from the weeds, causing them to die.

When growing garden plants from seed, wait until the crop emerges and grows taller than the barrier, then place the barrier alongside and around the plants. You also can use this method with transplants, by applying the barrier first and then planting the transplants through an opening cut into the barrier. Cut each opening in an "X" shape, so that as the transplant stem grows in diameter, the opening expands, and the plant is not constrained.

Using barriers to control diseases

Many diseases, such as black spot, produce spores on fallen leaves, which are splashed up onto the plant during rains or irrigation. Materials such as black plastic and weed barrier fabric keep infested fallen leaves and other plant parts from contacting the soil, thereby reducing the pathogens' ability to produce spores and re-infest the plants that season. Mulches are typically less effective

Soil solarization

Using radiation from the sun, *soil solarization* eliminates pathogens, insect eggs, and germinating weeds in the soil. Sunny weather is required, with daytime high temperatures averaging at least 85° Fahrenheit (29.4° Celsius). To treat an area, follow these steps:

1. Till, smooth, and irrigate the area of soil to be treated.
2. Cover the entire area with a clear plastic tarp, burying the edges of the plastic under the soil so that trapped heat cannot escape. The temperature under the plastic will reach at least 140° Fahrenheit (60° Celsius).
3. Leave the soil covered in this manner for at least four weeks to eliminate essentially all of the weed seeds in the top 1 inch of soil, as well as most disease pathogens and insects.
4. When planting, avoid working the soil so that weed seeds more than 1 inch deep are not brought to the soil surface where they will germinate.

Note that insects and pathogens more than 1 inch deep are still likely to attack the plants, particularly as roots grow deeper into the soil.

than plastic or weed barriers because mulches retain moisture and may provide a substrate for the continual survival of the pathogen.

Some disease-causing fungi can function as *saprophytes*, meaning that they live on dead material. It is possible for pathogens to be brought into the home landscape on mulches and grow saprophytically, building up enough inoculum to attack living plants. On the other hand, some fungi in mulches that function *only* as saprophytes, may outcompete pathogenic fungi trying to live in the mulch, and eliminate them.

Using barriers to control insects and mollusks

Barriers can manage insect pests and slugs by keeping them from reaching the host plant. For example, cabbage maggot (*Delia radicum*) feeds on the roots of cabbage, radish, broccoli, and many other vegetables. To lay their eggs in the soil near susceptible plants, the adult flies apparently must touch the soil directly. Materials such as window screening, weed barrier fabric, black plastic, or aluminum foil laid adjacent to the plants prevents flies from laying eggs, resulting in fewer maggots and less plant injury.

Floating row covers

Effective at keeping insect pests away from garden plants, floating row covers are made of spun bonded polyester fabrics that let water and most sunlight in. Although they are light enough to be laid on top of plants without harming them, wire hoops are also available to support the fabric above the plants. Keep the covers in place with long ground staples thrust through the edge of the material and into the soil. Place soil on the edge of the row cover to seal it. This will keep out many insect pests, including root maggots, leafminers, and cucumber beetles.

The striped cucumber beetle (*Acalymma vittatum*) transmits bacterial wilt to cucumbers and other cucurbit crops. In the spring, it is strongly attracted to cucurbits, particularly seedlings just emerging from the soil. Row covers placed over the plants will keep the beetles off the seedlings and protect the plants as they grow. If there is a large beetle population, enough beetles may tunnel through the soil to transmit the disease.

Once standard cucumbers begin to bloom, the row cover must be removed to allow bees and other insects to pollinate the flowers. Although striped cucumber beetles will then attack the plants and transmit disease, it will take several weeks for the disease to harm the plant. Fortunately, this is long enough for a large crop to be produced. 'Sweet Success' and several other cucumber varieties grown primarily for greenhouse production are *self-fertile*, meaning that they do not rely on pollination for cucumber production. These varieties can be kept covered for the entire growing season, with the cover opened only for weed control and harvest, as shown in figure 20.

Other useful barriers

Barriers also prevent black cutworms from attacking tomato and other transplants. Any type of barrier that extends 1 inch into the soil, protrudes at least 2 inches above the soil surface, and surrounds the plant will protect it. Effective barriers include strips of cardboard formed into a circle and held with a paper clip, tin cans and cardboard and plastic milk containers with tops and bottoms removed (as shown in figure 21), and various other objects. Another

Figure 20. Floating row cover placed over 'Sweet Success' cucumber to provide protection from striped cucumber beetles and associated bacterial wilt. Photo courtesy of Philip L. Nixon

Figure 21. Tin-can barrier protects a tomato transplant from black cutworm damage. Photo courtesy of Philip L. Nixon

method is to push a thick nail or small dowel into the soil against the transplant stem. This makes the stem too thick for the cutworm to curl its abdomen around the stem to feed.

A variety of barriers repel slugs and snails but may eventually ruin the soil for growing plants or make it difficult to do hand work in the garden. Salt, wood ashes, lime, sharp-edged gravel, and broken glass are examples. Copper barriers are a better choice. Insert strips of copper at least 1 inch into the soil, making sure they are wide enough to protrude at least 1 inch above the soil surface. The strips of copper generate a small electrical charge, and slugs and snails that touch the barrier receive an electrical shock and are repelled.

Chapter 7

Conventional and Biorational Pest Control Materials

Chemical management of pests in landscapes involves the use of pest control materials including insecticides, miticides, fungicides, and bactericides. Pest control materials are classified in a couple of ways: They can be contact or systemic; and they can be synthetically derived (made by humans, and often referred to as conventional), or biorational.

Contact and systemic pest control materials

Because contact pest control materials kill pests directly through physical contact, the effectiveness of these materials depends on thorough spray coverage. In addition, contact materials with short residual properties may require repeat applications.

Systemic pest control materials are applied to the leaves, stem, or soil. In general, the active ingredient is taken up and moved throughout the plant in the water-conducting tissues (xylem), food-conducting tissues (phloem), or both. Systemic controls generally take longer to work but last longer than contact controls because they are less susceptible to breakdown from rainfall or sunlight. Systemic insecticides are primarily effective against sucking insects such as aphids, whiteflies, mealybugs, and soft scales.

Contact and systemic fungicides are also available for foliar and soil-borne diseases. In addition, contact and systemic herbicides are available to manage grassy and broadleaf weeds. Exercise caution when using herbicides around desired plant material.

Conventional pest control materials

Conventional pest control materials are widely available to the general public at nurseries and garden centers. These synthetic controls include many insecticides, miticides, and fungicides. Most conventional pest control materials have a narrow or site-specific mode of activity. The *mode of activity* is how the active ingredient of a pest control material kills a given pest, whether it is an insect, a mite, or a disease—either by disrupting a particular target site or by negatively affecting a specific biological system.

For example, certain insecticides commonly used in landscapes and gardens are active on the nervous system of insects by blocking the action of specific enzymes (for example, acetylcholinesterase), nerve transport receptor sites, or nerve transmissions, thus causing insects to lose control of their nerve functions. These insecticides work on humans in the same manner, because humans and insects share certain nervous system characteristics.

Biorational pest control materials

Generally more environmentally sound than synthetically derived pest control materials, biorational pest control materials include bacteria, insect growth regulators (IGRs), insecticidal soap, horticultural oil, and botanicals. The most

Read and follow the pest control label

Always read the label carefully before applying any pest control material. The label contains important warnings and information, including the suggested application rate, target pests, plant types harmed, and proper precautions to take when making applications. Never use a pest control material for any purpose except those specifically listed on the label, and keep the phone number for your local poison center handy. The label is the law. Any misuse of a pest control material may lead to harmful effects to you or others, or to the treated plants (phytotoxicity). Always follow the label directions.

widely used bacterial insecticides are those containing *Bacillus thuringiensis* (Bt) toxins, because they have short residual activity and are specific to certain types of insects.

For Bt to work, the insect must eat materials containing it. Because products containing Bt are rapidly broken down by ultraviolet light, repeat applications may be necessary. These materials are important components of an IPM program because they generally have minimal impact on the natural enemies of pests, including beneficial insects and mites.

IGRs are used to control certain insect pests, including aphids, whiteflies, mealybugs, and scales. IGRs keep insect pests in a young stage or cause them to molt prematurely. These substances have no direct activity on adult insects but may cause adult females to lay infertile eggs.

Insecticidal soaps and horticultural oils are used in IPM programs because they have short residual activity and may have minimal impact on natural enemies of insect and mite pests. Both are contact controls. Insecticidal soaps kill insects and mites by disrupting cell membranes and causing desiccation (drying). Horticultural oils smother an insect's spiracles (breathing pores) and suffocate it. They have *broad-spectrum activity*, killing both active and over-wintering stages of insect and mite pests. In addition, horticultural oils are effective on certain foliar diseases, such as powdery mildew. Oils have been refined for use in summer as well as winter, although winter or dormant oil applications are usually of a higher oil concentration than summer oil applications.

Botanical or natural pest control materials are derived from plant parts. These are usually contact controls, and they tend to degrade quickly. Some

A caution about horticultural oils

When using horticultural oils, exercise caution: Making too many applications or applying when temperatures are above 80° Fahrenheit (26° Celsius) can result in plant damage. Avoid applying insecticidal soap and horticultural oil too frequently, that is more than twice within a seven-day period, as this may cause premature leaf drop or plants to burn. Some plants are very sensitive to oil sprays, and these are generally listed on the pesticide label.

botanical insecticides must be eaten by an insect or mite pest to be effective. Despite being classified as "natural," they may be just as toxic as synthetically derived pest control materials. Examples of botanical insect controls are nicotine, pyrethrin, rotenone, sabadilla, ryania, and neem. Neem is a widely used insecticide that acts as a repellent, anti-feedant (induces insects to stop feeding), and IGR.

Resistance

Avoid using the same insecticide/miticide continually year after year, as this can cause insect or mite pests to develop resistance, as demonstrated in figure 22. *Resistance* is the ability of a strain of insect or mite to tolerate or avoid factors that would prove lethal or impact reproduction in a normal population. It is the genetic ability of some individuals in a pest population to survive a pest control application. In other words, the material no longer effectively kills the target pest.

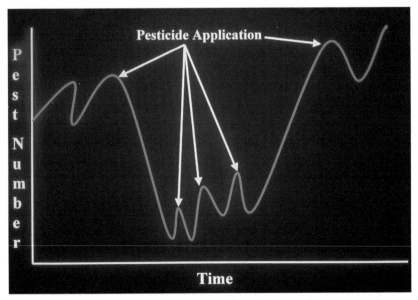

Figure 22. Diagram of pesticide resistance, showing increasing pest numbers over time with repeated pesticide applications. Courtesy of Raymond A. Cloyd

How insects and mites develop pesticide resistance

When a chemical causes high mortality, a result is the natural selection of individuals (insects and mites) that are less sensitive to the pesticide. This occurs primarily through the production of mutations, which have developed the genetic ability to tolerate applications of pest control materials. The rate at which insects or mites may develop resistance to pest control materials is influenced by the following factors:

- length of exposure (usually several years) to a single pest control material
- level of mortality (high versus low)
- presence or absence of refuge sites
- relatedness of one pest control material to another one
- generation time (short versus long)
- number of offspring (young) produced per generation
- mobility of individuals

To reduce the risk of pest populations developing resistance, follow these recommended guidelines:

- Use different insecticide/miticide types during the year—such as a bacterium, IGR, insecticidal soap, horticultural oil, or botanical.
- Implement IPM methods that minimize the use of pest control materials in landscapes and gardens.

For example, using high-pressure water sprays on a regular basis will preserve any natural enemies and can quickly knock down or kill soft-bodied insects such as aphids. Aphids knocked off plants with a hard stream of water usually leave their mouthparts in leaves or stems and therefore are unable to feed again. A hard water spray is also effective in knocking young lace bug nymphs off plants after they hatch from eggs.

Target pest resurgence and secondary pest outbreaks

Two pest situations can occur as a result of continual reliance on pest control materials to manage insect and mite pests in landscapes, and both are a result of killing natural enemies. These are target pest resurgence and secondary pest outbreaks. With *target pest resurgence*, an insect or mite pest population, after having been suppressed by the application of a pest control material, rebounds to numbers even higher than before suppression occurred (demonstrated in figure 23).

With *secondary pest outbreaks*, or pest replacement, a major pest is suppressed and continues to be suppressed by a particular pest-management tactic, such as the use of a pest control material, but is replaced in importance by another pest that was previously of minor status (demonstrated in figure 24). For example, heavy use of pest control materials such as carbaryl (Sevin) or cyfluthrin (Tempo) for managing Japanese beetle adults (shown feeding on a linden tree, *Tilia*, in plate 121) may create future problems with twospotted spider mites (*Tetranychus urticae*, shown in plates 122 and 123).

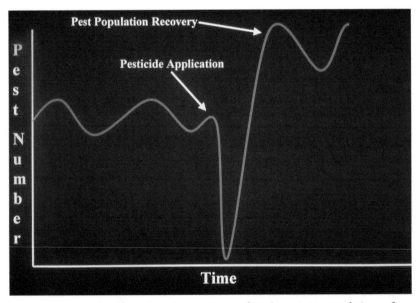

Figure 23. Diagram of target pest resurgence, showing a pest population, after having been suppressed by the application of a pest control material, rebounding to even higher numbers. Courtesy of Raymond A. Cloyd

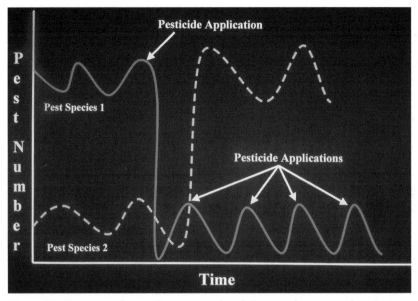

Figure 24. Diagram of secondary pest outbreak/pest replacement, showing a major pest suppressed by the use of a pest control material but replaced in importance by another pest previously of minor status. Courtesy of Raymond A. Cloyd

The role of natural enemies

Carbaryl and cyfluthrin are each very effective in managing the adult stage of Japanese beetle; however, both of these pest control materials have broad-spectrum activity, meaning that they kill many types of insects and mites. As a result, they are also harmful to natural enemies, including predatory insects and mites that naturally regulate twospotted spider mite populations. In the absence of these predatory insects and mites, twospotted spider mites can increase in numbers sufficient to cause plant injury. Because natural enemy populations take much longer to build up in numbers to have any influence on the mite populations, pest control materials will be needed regularly to prevent twospotted spider mite injury to plants.

Secondary pest outbreaks can occur in home landscape settings subsequent to applications of pest control material materials. For example, spraying malathion for mosquito control in residential areas can lead to outbreaks of pine needle scale (*Chionaspis pinifoliae*) on mugo pine (*Pinus mugo*, shown in plate 124), because malathion sprays kill the natural enemies of the scale.

Impact of pest control materials on natural enemies

Although pest control materials are effective in managing many plant-feeding insects and mites in landscapes and gardens, they may disrupt the natural balance by removing natural enemies, and thus increase the time required for re-colonization. This can lead to outbreaks of pests because pest species are generally less susceptible to pest control materials than natural enemies are. Frequent applications of conventional pest control materials can reduce natural enemy populations beyond recovery and cause repeated outbreaks of pest species.

Because natural enemy populations typically lag behind pest populations, natural enemy populations cannot increase until pest densities reach sufficient levels. This occurs primarily because spraying pest control materials, in particular contact insecticides, reduces populations of both pests and natural enemies. This then increases the numbers or the rate of increase in the surviving pest population due to reduced regulation by natural enemies. Furthermore, any remaining natural enemies may have difficulty finding prey, which then reduces their rate of increase.

Direct exposure versus indirect exposure

Pest control materials may impact the population of natural enemies either directly or indirectly. *Direct exposure* to a pest control spray kills the natural enemies that were initially present, because the natural enemies lack detoxifying enzymes, which are responsible for breaking down the pest control active ingredient into nonharmful molecules. These enzymes are generally more prevalent in pest populations.

Indirect exposure occurs when natural enemies starve to death because their food source is removed. In addition to the active ingredient, some other components of certain pest control materials, such as carriers, diluents, or inert ingredients, may be harmful to natural enemies. Furthermore, spray residues may be toxic to natural enemies or negatively impact them. For example, certain pyrethroid-based pest control materials have repellent activity, and spray residues may prevent natural enemies from reestablishing in landscapes.

Systemic pest control materials are generally considered less harmful to natural enemies because (a) there are minimal problems with spray drift and (b) the active ingredient is distributed throughout the plant and to plant parts where natural enemies are not exposed. However, systemic pest control materials may indirectly impact natural enemies by removing their food source or affecting natural enemies, such as predatory bugs (like the one shown in plate 125) that feed on plants in the absence of prey (food). Both of these situations may result in reducing natural enemies within a given area or impact their ability to maintain pest populations below damaging levels, by influencing their reproductive capacity or ability to search for food.

Botanical pest control materials, although considered "safer" than conventional pest control materials, can negatively affect natural enemies. For example, ryania, which is minimally harmful to predators, is extremely toxic to parasitoids.

Even fungicides such as sulfur (lime sulfur) can impact parasitoid and predator populations. For example, although sulfur has no activity on oyster-shell scale, it is highly toxic to the natural enemies of the scale. Also, fungicides used to manage apple scab may indirectly affect natural enemies.

Although it is essential to know how pest control materials impact natural enemies, it is equally important to understand how biological control is influenced by the interaction between plants, pests, and natural enemies. For example, when spider mites are not controlled or managed by either natural enemies or pest control materials, the mites can reach densities sufficient to defoliate the plants on which they are feeding. Spider mite densities often drop dramatically after defoliation. When plants produce new leaves, such outbreaks may be repeated. However, a small number of natural enemies of the spider mite may not survive under such conditions, primarily because the natural enemies don't have time to increase in sufficient numbers to influence the spider mite population and thus prevent plant injury. As a result, the use of a pest control material may be warranted.

The use of any pest control material should be based on an assessment of the pest problem and the potential impact on the natural enemies in the home landscape.

Chapter 8

Biological Pest Management

In long-established natural landscapes where there is minimal disturbance, such as forests or prairies, natural control is normally responsible for keeping pest populations in check. *Natural control* is the maintenance of a population of individuals (such as an insect or mite pest) over a relatively long period at a given level, through the combined effects of density-independent factors (environmental processes) and density-dependent factors on population growth and reduction. *Density* in this context refers to the number of pests in a given area (for example, 50 grubs per square foot or 100 aphids per foot of terminal growth).

Factors that impact pest populations

Characteristic abundance

The relatively constant population level that an insect or mite maintains over the long term, due primarily to regulatory processes in the environment is called the *characteristic abundance* (demonstrated in figure 25). Any disturbance—such as the application of a pest control material or a change in climate—will disrupt this population pattern. If these changes are severe and long lasting, then the characteristic abundance may not be reestablished.

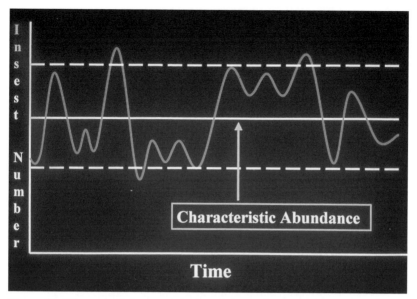

Figure 25. Diagram of characteristic abundance—the approximate size of a pest population maintained over the long term, due primarily to regulatory processes in the environment. Courtesy of Raymond A. Cloyd

Regulation versus control

Pest populations in a landscape may be either regulated or controlled. *Regulation* is the tendency of a pest population to sustain its characteristic abundance through density-dependent factors. This means that despite environmental disturbances (for example, weather), a given population will generally return to its characteristic abundance. *Control*, on the other hand, is the containment of a pest population within broad or narrow limits of fluctuation—often through some artificial intervention, such as the use of conventional pest control materials.

Density independence versus density dependence

Pest populations may be regulated naturally in landscapes either through density-independent factors or density-dependent factors. With *density-independent factors*, the effect or disturbance on a given population is entirely independent of the pest population (demonstrated in figure 26). Examples include

- use of pest control materials
- weather extremes
- change of seasons
- use of plants that are tolerant of insect and mite pests (that is, host plant resistance)

With *density-dependent factors*, the effect or disturbance changes in intensity along with population density. Examples include competition for food and shelter among a pest population, and the impact of natural enemies.

As the number of individuals in a pest population increases, the influence of density-dependent factors also increases. Both density-independent and density-dependent factors are continually acting on pest populations in landscapes. In habitats that contain more diverse plant communities, insect and mite pests may experience higher mortality from natural enemies.

Types of natural controls

In addition to climate, the primary natural controls responsible for regulating pest populations in landscapes are natural enemies, or biological control agents. The biological management of pests involves the use of *natural enemies* —living organisms such as parasitoids, predators, and pathogens (examples of which are shown in plates 126 through 128)—to manage pests in landscapes. Table 3 lists a variety of natural enemies that attack insect and mite pests in landscapes and gardens.

Parasitoids

Although parasitoids do not kill insects immediately, they do weaken them and reduce their ability to feed or reproduce. In biological control, female parasitoids are more important than males because they are responsible for attacking prey. The primary role of males is to fertilize females. Female parasitoids insert their eggs into insects, and the eggs hatch into young larvae. The larvae consume the insect's insides, and then mature into adults that eat a hole

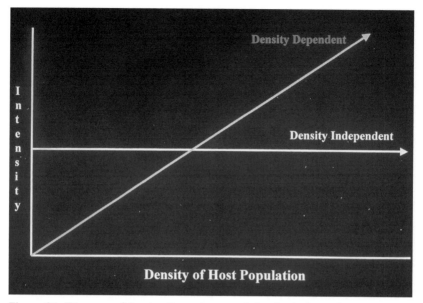

Figure 26. Diagram of density dependence and density independence. Density dependence indicates changes in population intensity due to a disturbance. Density independence indicates that a population effect or disturbance is not influenced by the population. Courtesy of Raymond A. Cloyd

in the dead insect and fly away (shown in plates 129 through 132). Some parasitoid adult females feed on prey or hosts to obtain food or to test the quality of the prey for egg laying. Even if the host is not selected, the feeding wound that the female creates may weaken the host so that it is unable to feed or reproduce.

Parasitic wasps and flies attack plant-feeding insects in home landscapes. Many parasitoids tend to be specific (specialists) in the types of insects that they attack and even the stage of insect they attack. For example, *Trichogramma* species parasitoids are very small and only attack insect eggs; other parasitoids attack only larvae, pupae, or both larvae and pupae.

Pathogens

Pathogens such as bacteria, fungi, and nematodes (shown in plate 133) work similarly to parasitoids in that they use the insect pest as a food source, eating

Table 3. Natural enemies found in landscapes and gardens, and the insect and mite pests they attack.

Natural enemies	Pests
Parasitoids	
Aphidius spp.	aphids
braconid wasps	aphids, caterpillars, and beetle larvae
Diaeretiella rapae	aphids
Encarsia formosa	whiteflies
ichneumon wasps	caterpillars, sawfly larvae, and beetle larvae
midges	aphids
tachinid wasps	caterpillars, sawfly larvae, squash bugs, stink bugs, and grasshoppers
Trichogramma spp.	caterpillar eggs
Predators	
assassin bugs	caterpillars and beetles
bigeyed bugs	aphids, leafhoppers, plant bugs, spider mites, and small caterpillars
damsel bugs	aphids, thrips, plant bugs, leafhoppers, and small caterpillars

the internal contents. Pathogens may enter an insect in a few different ways, namely by

- penetrating the cuticle
- being consumed or ingested during feeding
- entering through natural openings, including the spiracles (breathing pores), mouth, or anus

Although they do not kill the insect pest quickly, they do reduce feeding and reproduction. Examples of pathogens that kill insects include the soil-borne bacterium *Bacillus thuringiensis* (Bt) and the fungus *Beauveria bassiana*.

Table 3 continued.

Natural enemies	Pests
green lacewings	caterpillar eggs, small caterpillars, thrips, aphids, leafhopper nymphs, whiteflies, scales, mealybugs, and spider mites
ground beetles	beetle larvae, caterpillars, plant bugs, snails, slugs, and fly larvae
hover flies	aphids
ladybird beetles	aphids, whiteflies, spider mites, scales, mealybugs, and lace bug nymphs
minute pirate bugs	thrips, spider mites, aphids, small caterpillars, and leafhopper nymphs
predatory mites	spider mites and thrips
robber flies	beetles, leafhoppers, and plant bugs
rove beetles	aphids, spider mites, slugs, snails, and fly larvae
soldier beetles	aphids, caterpillars, beetles, beetle larvae, and grasshopper eggs
spined soldier bugs	caterpillars, sawfly larvae, and beetle larvae

Predators

Faster acting than parasitoids and pathogens, predators may eat a portion of an insect or the entire insect. They generally feed on all insect stages, including eggs, young, and adults. Plate 134 shows a ladybird beetle larvae eating a cottony cushion scale (*Icerya purchasi*).

A very large diversity of predator types exists in home landscapes and gardens—including praying mantids, katydids, dragonflies, damselflies, wasps, beetles, flies, lacewings, mites, true bugs, earwigs, thrips, and ants—some of which are shown in plates 135 through 146. Ants tend to protect colonies of sucking insects including aphids and soft scales from natural enemies, even moving aphids around on plants (plate 147 shows ants tending scale). However, ants are very efficient predators, especially in turfgrass habitats, where they feed on the eggs of certain species of soil-dwelling grub pests, including Japanese beetle.

Despite the benefits of having predators in home landscapes, it is important to realize that many predators are generalists and will attack and consume beneficial insects and mites as well as pests. A combination of both types of natural enemies—parasitoids and predators—in home landscapes helps to maintain a balance in managing plant-feeding insects and mites.

Biological control approaches: augmentation and conservation

Augmentation is biological control in which natural enemies are introduced to control an existing pest population. Plate 148 shows purchased containers of biological controls for this purpose. The two augmentation strategies are:

- *Inoculation* is the release of low numbers of natural enemies over a long time. Offspring or young produced from the released individuals provide continued control.
- *Inundation* is the release of large numbers of natural enemies to reduce the pest population quickly. This strategy does not rely on offspring or young to provide additional or continued control, and the reduction of pest numbers is similar to that achieved with an insecticide.

A problem when releasing purchased natural enemies such as ladybird beetle adults, shown in plate 149, is that the beetles may leave the release area in search of prey even though prey still exists in the release area. In general, parasitoids and predators do not find and attack every single pest, particularly if the pests are at low densities. Instead, they often leave to find areas were prey is more abundant.

Conservation biological control preserves, protects, attracts, and retains existing populations of natural enemies. You can accomplish this by

- growing plants that attract natural enemies and provide a food source, such as pollen and nectar (refer to table 4 for examples)
- reducing the use of conventional pest control materials

Using trap crops to preserve natural enemies

Trap crops are plants—generally located around the perimeter of the landscape or garden—that attract insect pests, which then act as a food reservoir for natural enemies. When the numbers of prey decline on the main plants, the natural enemies can migrate back to the trap crop. For example, sweet alyssum (*Lobularia maritima*) which is very attractive to aphids, can serve as a supplemental food source for many parasitoids and predators. Because aphid species are typically specific in feeding on only a few types of plants, these aphids are unlikely to be pests on landscape or garden plants.

Honeydew as a food source for parasitoids

Produced by sucking insects such as aphids, soft scales, and mealybugs, honeydew may be a food source during spring for parasitoids that use sucking insects as a host. However, it is an inadequate food source during summer because it dries out quickly and is lower in quality. Furthermore, honeydew is an excellent growing medium for sooty mold fungi, which can reduce a plant's aesthetic appeal.

- reducing the frequency of conventional pest control applications
- using pest control materials that are less harmful to natural enemies, such as bacterial toxins.

The benefits of a diverse landscape

Diverse or complex landscapes, which contain a variety of plant types including flowers, shrubs, and trees (as shown in figure 27), tend to have higher rates of natural enemies (particularly parasitic wasps) than simple landscapes do. For example, the aphid parasitoid *Diaeretiella rapae* has an attack rate of 29.3 percent in diverse landscapes but an attack rate of only 3.7 percent in

Table 4. Plants within various plant families that are useful in landscapes and gardens for attracting natural enemies

---

Brassicaceae (mustard family)

basket-of-gold alyssum	*Aurinium saxatilis*
candytuft	*Iberis* spp.
hoary alyssum	*Berteroa incana*
mustards	*Brassica* spp.
sweet alyssum	*Lobularia maritima*
yellow rocket	*Barbarea vulgaris*
wild mustard	*Brassica kabe*

Compositae (aster family)

blanketflower	*Gaillardia* spp.
blazing star	*Liatris* spp.
coneflower	*Echinacea* spp.
coreopsis	*Coreopsis* spp.
cosmos	*Cosmos bipinnatus*
golden marguerite	*Anthemis tinctoria*
goldenrod	*Solidago* spp.
sunflower	*Helianthus* spp.
tansy	*Tanacetum vulgare*
yarrow	*Achillea* spp.

---

simple landscapes. Furthermore, the rate of parasitism increases with the abundance and variety of wildflowers. For example, the parasitism rate is as much as 18 times higher on tent caterpillar pupae in areas with abundant undergrowth of wildflowers, when compared with areas where few wildflowers are present.

Diverse landscapes, including those with turfgrass, also experience far fewer insect and mite outbreaks, because there tends to be a rich abundance of natural enemies that maintain pest populations below damaging levels. In

Table 4 continued.

Leguminosae (pea family)

alfalfa	*Medicago sativa*
big flower vetch	*Vicia* spp.
broad bean	*Vicia faba*
hairy vetch	*Vicia villosa*
sweet clover	*Melilotus* spp.

Umbelliferae (carrot family)

bishop's weed	*Ammi majus*
caraway	*Carum carvi*
coriander	*Coriandrum sativum*
dill	*Anethum graveolens*
fennel	*Foeniculum vulgare*
Queen Anne's lace (wild carrot)	*Daucus carota*
bisnaga	*Ammi visnaga*
wild parsnip	*Pastinaca sativa*

Other plants

baby blue eyes	*Nemophila menziesii*
buckwheat	*Fagopyrum esculentum*
cinquefoil	*Potentilla* spp.
milkweeds	*Asclepias* spp.

fact, in a diverse landscape that is not intensively maintained, turfgrass provides the benefit of higher populations of predators, because ants, ground beetles, rove beetles, and even spiders are more common in turfgrass habitats (refer to figure 28). These predators can provide control of certain turfgrass pests. For example, ground-nesting ants will attack sod webworm larvae, and ground beetles will feed on armyworm pupae. One type of natural enemy may not always be able to regulate pest populations, because the reproductive capacity of the pest far exceeds the ability of the natural enemy to regu-

Figure 27. Incorporating a diversity of different plants into a landscape will attract and retain natural enemies. Photo courtesy of Raymond A. Cloyd

late the pest population and prevent plant injury. This is why having a diverse or complex landscape is important, as many different types of natural enemies are present.

The benefits of flowers

Plants with flowers, including wildflowers (particularly those with yellow or orange flowers), that are incorporated into landscapes provide mating sites for natural enemies and sites for alternative larval hosts and prey, as well as promote immigration into the landscape. Flowers provide essential food for natural enemies that ensures their survival, but they also influence reproductive capacity and natural enemy longevity. To retain natural enemies in a landscape or garden, it is important to have both annual and perennial plants

Figure 28. A maintained lawn is more susceptible to insect attack than less intensively maintained turf in a complex landscape. Photo courtesy of Philip L. Nixon

blooming throughout the growing season so that an abundant food supply for natural enemies is readily available.

It is also critical for flowers to be accessible to natural enemies. *Floral architecture*, which is the arrangement of petals, stamens, and other flower parts, determines the accessibility of nectar glands to natural enemies. For an insect to readily obtain pollen and nectar from a flower, the flower's architecture must be compatible with the insect's morphology and flower-foraging behavior. Thus, certain flower types may be more accessible as a food source. Plants in the family *Umbelliferae*, such as dill (*Anethum graveolens*) and fennel (*Foeniculum vulgare*), are suitable food sources for many parasitoids and predators because these plant types have exposed nectarines (nectar-producing glands). Parasitioids tend to feed more on flowers with exposed nectaries because of the easier access to pollen and nectar. Parasitoids such as ichneumon wasps may feed on setae (hairs) present on the leaves and flowers of certain plant types.

How cultural practices impact biological control

The abundance of natural enemies in landscapes also depends on whether plants are located in the sun or shade. Natural enemies tend to be more numerous in shady locations with a diversity of plantings, because the environmental conditions, including moderate temperatures and higher humidity, are more favorable to survival and reproduction. For example, azalea lace bug populations are lower and cause less injury to azaleas planted in shade than to those planted in sun because of the higher numbers and greater variety of natural enemies in shady locations.

Planting trees in landscapes can result in increased populations of natural enemies. For example, the drip line or border of trees provides food (prey), shelter, and refuge for predators, especially during environmental stress. Populations of ladybird beetles and green lacewings are higher in tree borders.

The application of fertilizers, particularly those high in nitrogen, can favorably impact the success of natural enemies, because plant nutritional quality plays a role in plant-feeding insects' vulnerability to natural enemies. The low nutrient value of underfertilized plants may actually lengthen the developmental period for immature stages of insect pests. This results in higher pest mortality, because the vulnerable stage is exposed to parasitoids and predators for longer periods of time.

On the other hand, some parasitoids may prefer to attack prey feeding on plants that contain high nitrogen concentrations, because the prey is of higher nutrient value, thus ensuring survival of young. Plant nitrogen concentrations also may influence the sex ratio (females to males) of parasitoids, because higher proportions of female parasitoids (the preferred sex) generally emerge from prey that have fed on plants containing high nitrogen concentrations. This may be a result of prey size, because larger prey generally produce a greater proportion of females.

Chapter 9

Insect and Disease Associations

A number of insect species that attack plants in landscapes are also vectors of several diseases destructive to trees, shrubs, and herbaceous plants. Insect-vectored diseases that affect landscape plants include:

- aster yellows (unnamed phytoplasma)
- oak wilt (*Ceratocystis fagacearum*)
- Dutch elm disease (*Ophiostoma ulmi*)
- elm phloem necrosis (elm yellows, unnamed phytoplasma)
- pine wilt (pinewood nematode, *Bursaphelenchus xylophilus*)
- rose rosette (unknown, virus suspect)
- ash yellows (unnamed phytoplasma)
- bacterial leaf scorch (*Xyella fastidiosa*)

In addition, insects such as ambrosia beetles are associated with harmful fungi. The primary means of dealing with these insect-vectored diseases is through prevention and sanitation.

Aster yellows

A disease caused by a phytoplasma (a microorganism formerly called a mycoplasma-like organism), aster yellows is spread by phloem-feeding insects. Phytoplasmas are similar to bacteria in size and in that they contain cytoplasm, reproduce by fission, and are sensitive to antibiotics. They are similar to viruses in that they cannot be grown in culture, lack a cell wall, and cause virus-like symptoms. They are limited to the phloem tissues and are therefore systemic in the host plant.

Symptoms of aster yellows infection vary depending on the host plant but may include

- yellowing leaves (chlorosis)
- dwarfing of plants
- proliferation of adventitious buds, resulting in bushy growth resembling witches' broom
- small flowers or flowers with partially green petals

Plants infected early may die before reaching maturity.

The disease has a wide range of potential hosts, including *Campanula*, *Chrysanthemum*, *Coreopsis*, *Delphinium*, marigold (*Tagetes*), pansy (*Viola*), *Petunia*, and *Salvia*, and the phytoplasma overwinters in weeds and ornamental plants.

The aster leafhopper (*Macrosteles quadrilineatus*) and several other leafhoppers are vectors of aster yellows. Leafhoppers acquire the phytoplasma along with plant fluids while feeding on the food-conducting tissues (phloem) of infected plants. The phytoplasma incubates for a specific period of time inside the insect's gut. When the leafhopper feeds on healthy (uninfected) plants, the phytoplasma is inserted through the mouthparts into the phloem, where it multiplies and establishes infection.

Management of aster yellows involves controlling leafhopper vectors. However, this is not always feasible, in particular with very large plants. Removing symptomatic plants and removing weeds, which serve as reservoirs for the phytoplasma, will help to eliminate sources of inoculum.

Oak wilt

A systemic fungal disease, oak wilt primarily kills trees in the red-black oak group, including

- black oak (*Quercus velutina*)
- red oak (*Q. rubra*)

- pin oak (Q. *palustris*)
- scarlet oak (Q. *coccinea*)
- shingle oak (Q. *imbricaria*)

It is less likely to kill trees in the white-bur oak group:

- white oak (Q. *alba*)
- bur oak (Q. *macrocarpa*)
- post oak (Q. *stellata*)
- swamp oak (Q. *bicolor*)
- chinquapin oak (Q. *prinoides*)

The disease plugs the water-conducting tissues (xylem), preventing the absorption of water. This results in leaf wilting, branch dieback, and eventually death of infected trees. The primary vectors of the oak wilt fungus are oak bark beetles and sap-feeding beetles.

Oak wilt is spread by underground root grafts or by insects aboveground. Sometimes fungal mats form beneath the bark of trees killed by the wilt fungus. Spores produced on these mats adhere to the body of sap beetles when they walk over and feed on the fungal mats. The beetles then fly to healthy trees, where they feed on plant sap oozing from fresh wounds. The fungus enters trees through feeding wounds created by the beetles.

Bark beetles breed in recently killed trees. Adults that emerge from trees killed by the fungus are usually contaminated with fungal spores. The contaminated adults then migrate to healthy oak trees and feed within cavities that they create in twigs, thus transmitting the fungus.

Once trees are infected with the fungus, management is difficult and may be costly. Removing dead and dying trees is imperative to prevent spread to healthy trees. Be sure to sever root grafts between diseased and healthy trees before removing any diseased trees. Avoid keeping diseased oaks for firewood, because the firewood may not be burned before the following spring, when beetles emerge and may carry the fungus to healthy trees. Also avoid pruning oaks when beetles are active, which is primarily from May through July. Pruning creates wounds with sap flow, which may attract beetles. It is best to prune during the dormant season or late summer. Systemic fungicides may be used to protect nearby healthy trees.

Dutch elm disease

The fungus that causes the destructive Dutch elm disease is responsible for the decline of American elm trees (*Ulmus americana*) throughout the United States. Many other elm species are also susceptible. The disease may move upward and downward within plants, plugging the water-conducting tissues (xylem). This causes wilting of branches near the top of trees (also known as "flagging"), branch dieback, and eventually death of the tree. The native elm bark beetle (*Hylurgopinus rufipes*) and the smaller European elm bark beetle (*Scolytus multistriatus*) are vectors of the Dutch elm disease fungus.

Both beetles are attracted to the volatile chemicals that healthy elm trees produce. The native elm bark beetle primarily tunnels into the bark of branches and small twigs, whereas the smaller European elm bark beetle feeds on twigs, usually at the crotches. During feeding, the beetles deposit spores, which cause infection. The beetles aggregate in dead trees, using stems and branches as breeding sites. Egg-laying beetles tunnel into the cambium and sapwood of healthy trees. The fungus germinates inside egg galleries produced by the adult and larva within the bark. Beetles become contaminated with the fungus when they molt to adulthood, and the sticky spores attach to their bodies when they emerge. They then transport the fungus when they arrive at a new feeding site.

Managing Dutch elm disease relies on prevention, sanitation, and the use of resistant varieties of elm trees. Insecticides may be applied to the bark during peak beetle activity (March through May) to kill beetles before they deposit spores; however, this may not be feasible for large trees. Maintaining tree health through proper watering, fertility, mulching, and pruning may alleviate problems and possibly allow trees to defend themselves from infection. Pruning wounds tend to attract beetles, so prune during the dormant season.

The primary strategy for managing Dutch elm disease is to eliminate breeding sites such as dead trees or branches before beetles are attracted to infested, dying wood. In spring, monitor trees for symptoms of wilt: brown streaking on wood when the bark is removed. Pruning out infected branches may save trees only if done early in the infection process, when no more than 5 to 10 percent of the tree shows symptoms. It is essential to follow these precautions:

- Prune back approximately 10 feet from the point where the brown streaking stops.
- Disinfect pruning tools (such as saws) between cuts.
- Prune or trim affected branches and then burn or destroy the debris.
- Cut down and destroy trees that have died.

Wood cut during late fall or winter may be used as firewood, provided it is used before beetles emerge in the spring. Bark beetles can breed in piles of elm wood with attached bark. Remove and discard bark from firewood and cover it with black plastic to exclude the beetles.

Elm species that are resistant to Dutch elm disease (or tolerant of it) include Chinese elm (*Ulmus parvifolia*), Japanese elm, (*U. davidii* var. *japonica*) and Siberian elm (*U. pumila*). Several new varieties of American elm, including 'Valley Forge,' 'New Harmony,' and 'Independence' have demonstrated resistance.

Additional strategies include luring beetles into localized areas using either pheromone traps or "trap trees." Trap trees may be used to lure pests and then are either sprayed or cut down and disposed of. These trees, which are highly susceptible to a particular pest (beetle), can be used to monitor its population (for example, timing of attack). Systemic fungicides may be applied to infested trees with 5-percent infection or less, but it can be costly and require repeat applications.

Elm phloem necrosis

A serious disease of American elm (white elm), phloem necrosis or elm yellows also infects other elm species, but to a lesser degree. Symptoms of infection resemble those of Dutch elm disease—including rapid decline, which leads to death of infected trees. However, the vascular streaking typical of Dutch elm disease is absent with elm phloem necrosis. Trees typically die within a year after the onset of symptoms. The pathogen is a phytoplasma, similar to aster yellows, and the primary vector is the whitebanded elm leafhopper (*Scaphoideus luteolus*).

The leafhopper acquires the phytoplasma by removing plant fluids from the phloem of leaves and succulent stems of infected elms. After an incubation period of approximately three weeks, the leafhopper, which generally feeds along the mid-veins, is capable of transmitting the organism to healthy elms. Transmission generally occurs during July through September when leafhoppers are active. Once infected with the phytoplasma, the leafhopper is a potential vector for the remainder of its life. Other insects, including the meadow spittlebug (*Philaenus spumarius*), may transmit the pathogen.

Elm phloem necrosis is managed similarly to other insect-vectored diseases such as oak wilt and Dutch elm disease. Insecticide use may prevent feeding by leafhoppers but in most cases is ineffective in reducing disease transmission. Keeping plants healthy through proper watering, fertility, mulching, and pruning can help alleviate problems with the disease. The primary management strategy is to remove all dead and diseased trees and wood as soon as possible.

Pine wilt disease

A serious disease of pines, pine wilt involves an association between the pinewood nematode (*Bursaphelenchus xylophilus*) and the sawyer beetle (*Monochamus*). In addition to pine trees, certain other tree species may be susceptible to the disease, including:

- white spruce (*Picea glauca*)
- balsam fir (*Abies balsamea*)
- European larch (*Larix decidua*)
- atlas cedar (*Cedrus atlantica*)
- deodar cedar (*C. deodara*)

Trees that are at least ten years old are more likely to contract this disease, mainly because they are more attractive to the insect vector. Trees weakened by drought stress also are more susceptible to the beetles.

Typical symptoms of trees infected with pinewood nematodes include crown flagging and a gray-green color to needles. However, it may take a year for symptoms to be expressed. In the meantime, trees weakened by the disease may succumb to attack by secondary insects or diseases, but an infestation of pinewood nematode always results in tree death.

The disease vector is the sawyer beetle, classified as a long-horned beetle because of the length of its antennae. The beetle carries pinewood nematodes (microscopic roundworms) in its body from one tree to the next. The nematodes are the primary organisms responsible for causing tree injury.

Adult female beetles chew holes in dead or dying pines and then they lay one to two eggs in each site underneath the bark. The eggs hatch into legless, grublike, white larvae that have brown heads. Larvae feed between the bark, and then they tunnel deeper into the wood. The larvae are 0.75 to 1.5 inches long when full grown. They overwinter in the tunnels and pupate in the spring. When the beetle emerges from the pupae stage and hardens its cuticle (skin), the pinewood nematode, which is already present in the tree, enters the spiracles (breathing pores) of the beetle. Dead pines already infected with the nematodes may harbor millions of pinewood nematodes. The nematodes then congregate in the beetle's tracheae (breathing tubes). Beetles may have as many as 90,000 pinewood nematodes present in their tracheal system.

Adult beetles emerge from dead wood during late spring through late fall. They are 0.75 to 1.5 inches long and gray, brown, to black in color. The body is usually mottled with small, light-colored spots. The antennae, particularly the male antennae, can be as long as four times the body length. Adult beetles, which live up to four months, are active primarily at night and hide during the day in the tree canopy or on bark. There may be one or two generations per year. The adult beetles fly to live pines and feed on branches, usually the first- and second-year twigs.

The nematodes leave the beetle spiracles and enter the tree through the feeding wounds in the branches. Although nematodes may be distributed throughout the tree, they generally are not located in needles or cones, as these plant parts are too dry for nematode survival. The nematodes migrate to the resin canals of pine trees where they reproduce rapidly to very high numbers. They destroy the resin canals and plug the water transport system (xylem) of the tree. As a result, the needles of infested pine trees turn dull green and then brown. In addition to feeding on the resin canals, pinewood nematodes feed on blue stain fungi that are introduced into trees on the bodies of engraver beetles attracted to dying trees. This causes the nematodes to multiply rapidly. Depending on the level of nematode infestation, pine trees may die in less than one year. The nematodes can overwinter in both dead and live trees.

Managing pine wilt disease involves implementing proper sanitation procedures and cultural practices for plant health. Prune dead branches from live pine trees to reduce potential infestation by the beetle, always disinfecting the pruning tools after each tree. Seventy-percent isopropyl alcohol (rubbing alcohol) is one disinfectant option.

Remove all dead pines and replace them with trees that are less susceptible to the disease, such as Norway spruce (*Picea abies*), blue spruce (*P. pungens* f. *glauca*), Douglas fir (*Pseudotsuga menziesii*), or hemlock (*Tsuga*). Do not store any wood for firewood—either burn or bury it immediately. Maintaining tree health through proper watering, fertility, mulching, and pruning may alleviate problems and possibly enable trees to defend themselves.

Rose rosette

Caused by a double-stranded ribonucleic acid (RNA), rose rosette is generally considered to be a virus-like disease. Its symptoms are very distinct: the new growth, both leaves and stems, take on a deep red color. On hybrid tea roses, this growth may be lime colored. Leaves may be crinkled, distorted, or exhibit a mosaic pattern of green, yellow, and red. An infected plant produces numerous lateral shoots growing in different directions, giving the plant the appearance of witches' broom. These shoots are typically much larger in diameter than the original canes; and thorns on these stems are more numerous than normal, giving the stem an almost hairy appearance. Plants usually die within about twenty-two months of infection. Fortunately, rose rosette is often identified in the nursery, where infected plants can be removed before they make it into the retail market.

Multiflora rose (*Rosa multiflora*) is the most common host of this disease. Not surprisingly, in areas where this rose is common, the threat of disease is high. Rose rosette has been reported on cultivated flowering varieties as well. Climbers, hybrid teas, floribundas, miniatures, and a number of old-variety roses may be infected. Hosts other than roses have not been reported.

The vector of this pathogen is an eriophyid mite, *Phyllocoptes fructiphylus*. Eriophyid mites are minuscule—about one-third the size of spider mites, which are commonly visible on plants. You will need a strong magnifying lens to see eriophyid mites. Although they cannot fly, these mites can move about by crawling and travel long distances on wind currents. It is possible to spread rose rosette disease through grafting, but it cannot be spread mechanically, such as with pruning tools.

Because infected plants cannot be saved, it is important to dig up and destroy any plants (including roots) as soon as you notice symptoms of the disease. Planting multiflora and garden roses as far apart as possible is strongly recommended. The effectiveness of mite control may be questionable, but if you use it, apply it during the critical mite transmission time of May and June. The purpose of mite control is to prevent the disease by killing the mite and its eggs before the pathogen has spread.

Ash yellows

Although it primarily infects white and green ash (*Fraxinus americana* and *F. pennsylvanica*) in the north central and northeastern United States, ash yellows also infects other ash species and lilac (*Syringa*). The disease, caused by a phytoplasma, is characterized by a loss of tree vigor over two to ten years followed by tree death.

Symptoms include short internodes (spaces between nodes) and—due to the loss of older leaves—the appearance of clumps of foliage at branch ends. The leaves, which often are stunted and folded, become pale green to chlorotic (yellowed) and may develop fall colors prematurely. Infected trees may lose their leaves completely, but usually the canopy appears sparse. Cankers form on the branches and the trunk, leading to twig and branch dieback. Witches' broom sometimes appears on branches but is more common at the base of the trunk. Still, these brooms appear on only a small percentage of infected trees. Cracks may appear in this area of the trunk as well. It is rare for an ash tree to recover from ash yellows.

A large percentage of the ash trees grown in midwestern U.S. landscapes are green ash. Unfortunately, green ash trees do not show ash yellows symptoms as clearly as white ash trees do. With diseased green ash trees, the typical witches' broom and yellowing are not always apparent; however, cankers and stem dieback are common. Ash yellows symptoms on green ash may be easily confused with ash decline from verticillium wilt or non-infectious problems, such as moisture stress, compacted soil, and other site stress.

The ash yellows phytoplasma is moved from tree to tree by certain leafhoppers and spittlebugs. The brown speckled leafhopper (*Paraphlepsius irroratus*) and the meadow spittlebug (*Philaenus spumarius*) have been implicated in the spread of the ash yellows pathogen. Grafting as observed in nurseries can also spread the pathogen.

There are no known control measures to prevent or cure ash yellows. Once a tree has been diagnosed with ash yellows, cutting and removal of the infected tree is recommended.

Bacterial leaf scorch

The bacterium *Xylella fastidiosa* is responsible for bacterial leaf scorch, but it is very different from other bacterial plant pathogens. Bacterial leaf scorch is a fastidious, xylem-inhabiting bacterium (FXIB), found only in the xylem of host plants. It cannot be isolated on normal laboratory media, nor can it be seen with a compound microscope. Furthermore, the disease is difficult to confirm, as many strains of the bacterium exist. Although bacterial leaf scorch is a concern with trees, the pathogen responsible for it also has been reported in coffee, and causes:

- Pierce's disease of grape
- citrus variegated chlorosis
- phony peach disease
- alfalfa dwarf
- almond leaf scorch
- plum leaf scald
- periwinkle wilt
- oleander wilt

Some of these diseases can be extremely injurious to plants, if not lethal. Bacterial leaf scorch has been reported in many hosts, including:

- oak (*Quercus*): pin, red, scarlet, bur, white, willow, shingle
- maple (*Acer*): silver, sugar, red
- American elm (*Ulmus americana*)
- American sycamore (*Platanus occidentalis*)
- London planetree (*Platanus* ×*acerifolia*)
- hackberry (*Celtis*)
- sweetgum (*Liquidambar styraciflua*)
- red mulberry (*Morus rubra*)

It also has been found in certain weeds; however, it is unknown whether these weeds serve as an inoculum source.

The symptoms of bacterial leaf scorch on trees are similar to those of environmental scorch: the margins of the leaves become necrotic. Often, there is a slight yellow or red zone between healthy and affected tissue. Sometimes the brown tissue appears to have rings or zones that are darker. However, neither of those symptoms is always present. On some hosts, the older leaves are affected first and the youngest last; however, this does not hold true for oaks.

One constant is that the disease appears on a tree in mid to late summer, as opposed to early in the season when environmental scorch symptoms are likely to appear. In addition, the disease starts on one branch or area of the tree. The next season the tree forms normal-appearing leaves without scorch symptoms, but by mid to late summer, the symptoms are back, and more intense than the year before. This scenario is repeated for four to six years until the tree dies. Environmental scorch does not kill trees.

Bacterial leaf scorch may be spread by leafhoppers, possibly even by spittlebugs, and by root grafts. Disease spread is slow. Elms that are infected may be predisposed to attack by elm bark beetles, which are potential vectors of the fungus that causes Dutch elm disease.

We recommend monitoring trees for bacterial leaf scorch: keep notes on the progress of scorch symptoms in trees and evaluate whether site stress factors might be contributing to symptoms. If you have noted symptoms for longer than two years, then consider sampling the tree for laboratory testing when symptoms are intense during late summer. If the disease is confirmed, tree removal is an option, but does not appear to be necessary unless the tree is a potential hazard. If infection is not severe, try removing dead wood, disinfecting the cutting blades between cuts. It is likely that the tree will continue to decline and eventually die. Injections of antibiotics labeled for use on bacterial leaf scorch may be an option, but this seems only to suppress the disease. Furthermore, injections can be costly and will need to be repeated, possibly annually.

Ambrosia beetles

The name *ambrosia beetle* comes from the fact that it feeds on fungi called "ambrosia," although the beetle also is associated with a blue stain fungus responsible for reducing the quality of lumber. Male ambrosia beetles tunnel into wood first and create galleries consisting of small pinholes surrounded by a dark stain. Eventually, females join the males and construct most of the tunnels, and then lay eggs in the galleries. Larval development occurs primarily in these galleries. Ambrosia beetles culture blue stain fungi in their tunnels and use the fungal spores for food.

Female beetles transport blue stain fungi within specialized sacs, and the fungal spores proliferate within the body of the beetle. Inoculation into living plant tissue takes place after the tunnels reach the cambium region, at which point the fungus grows rapidly and interferes with plant transpiration by blocking water-conducting vessels.

Managing ambrosia beetles relies on a variety of strategies to prevent them from feeding on trees. Certain types of insecticides or repellents may be applied to trees to prevent feeding and disease transmission, but the feasibility of this approach depends on tree size. Because ambrosia beetles primarily attack stressed trees, maintaining plant health through proper watering, fertility, mulching, and pruning is the best way to prevent problems with them. Remove attacked dead or dying trees and dispose of the wood or burn it, as it serves as a breeding site for beetles. Another management option is mass trapping of beetles using a synthetic pheromone in combination with traps.

Chapter 10

Putting It All Together

The goal of this book has been to provide a broader view of IPM—to discuss how all of the components of IPM work together to prevent or minimize insect and disease problems in home landscapes and gardens.

We began by discussing the needs of plants, both aboveground and belowground, to maintain good health and ward off insect and disease pests. The best way to ensure plant health is to provide the proper cultural requirements, including careful plant selection and placement, watering, fertility, mulching, and pruning. Next, we explored the needs of insects, mites, diseases, and other organisms, in order to understand why certain IPM strategies are effective. The most important factors in implementing IPM strategies are (a) to recognize or identify the pest or pests causing the problem and (b) to assess whether there is a need for pest management tactics. This is accomplished by monitoring the number of pests present, time of year that pests are attacking plants, plant age, and location of the plants infested.

There are primarily four management strategies that define IPM—cultural, physical or mechanical, use of pest control materials, and biological—and several chapters discussed these strategies in detail. A single strategy or a combination of management strategies may be appropriate for preventing or reducing a particular pest problem. Each strategy has certain characteristics that validate its use in dealing with particular pests in landscapes and gardens. Sometimes, doing nothing is a much better long-term strategy than simply applying a pest control material, as pest control materials may disrupt the natural control provided by natural enemies. Certain insects and diseases maintain close associations that allow them to work together to attack plants, and these associations are critical to the survival of both organisms.

We hope that this basic knowledge of the components of IPM and how they are interconnected will help you to make better management decisions, and result in fewer problems with insects and diseases in your own home landscape and garden.

Appendix A

Suggested Reading

Agrios, G. N. 1997. *Plant Pathology*. 4th ed. San Diego, California: Academic Press.

Buczacki, S. 2000. *Plant Problems: Prevention and Control*. Devon, England: LEGO SpA, David and Charles, Brunnel House, and Newton Abbot.

Carr, A. 1979. *Rodale's Color Handbook of Garden Insects*. St. Emmaus, Pennsylvania: Rodale Press.

Carson, R. 1987. *Silent Spring*. Boston: Houghton Mifflin. (First published in 1962.)

Chase, A. R., M. Daughtrey, and G. W. Simone. 1995. *Diseases of Annuals and Perennials: Identification and Control*. Batavia, Illinois: Ball Publishing.

Controlling Pests and Diseases. 1994. St. Emmaus, Pennsylvania: Rodale Press.

Garden Pests and Diseases. 1993. Menlo Park, California: Sunset Publishing.

Hansen, E. M., and K. J. Lewis, eds. 1997. *Compendium of Conifer Diseases*. St. Paul, Minnesota: APS Press.

Hill, J. B., H. W. Popp, and A. R. Grove, Jr. 1967. *Botany: A Textbook for Colleges*. 4th ed. New York: McGraw-Hill.

Hopkins, W. G. 1999. *Introduction to Plant Physiology*. 2d ed. New York: John Wiley and Sons.

Horst, R. K., ed. 1983. *Compendium of Rose Diseases*. St. Paul, Minnesota: APS Press.

International Society of Arboriculture; University of Illinois. 1997. Plant Health Care for Woody Ornamentals. A Professional's Guide to Preventing and Managing Environmental Stresses and Pests. Savoy, Illinois: International Society of Arboriculture; Urbana-Champaign, Illinois:

171

Cooperative Extension Service, College of Agricultural, Consumer, and Environmental Sciences, University of Illinois.

Johnson, W. T., and H. H. Lyon. 1988. *Insects that Feed on Trees and Shrubs*. 2d ed. Ithaca, New York: Comstock Publishing Associates.

Jones, R. K., and D. M. Benson, eds. 2001. *Diseases of Woody Ornamentals and Trees in Nurseries*. St. Paul, Minnesota: APS Press.

Leslie, A. R., ed. 1994. *Handbook of Integrated Pest Management for Turf and Ornamentals*. London: CRC Press, Lewis Publishers.

Marinelli, J. ed. 1994. *Natural Insect Control: The Ecological Gardener's Guide to Foiling Pests*. Handbook no. 139. Brooklyn, New York: Brooklyn Botanic Gardens.

Marinelli, J., ed. 2000. *Natural Disease Control: A Common-Sense Approach to Plant First Aid*. Handbook no. 164. Brooklyn, New York: Brooklyn Botanic Gardens.

Olkowski, W. S. Daar, and H. Olkowski. 1991. *Common-Sense Pest Control*. Newtown, Connecticut: Taunton Press.

Organic Gardener's Handbook of Natural Insect and Disease Control. 1992. St. Emmaus, Pennsylvania: Rodale Press.

Otis, C. M., and T. D. Murray. 2001. *Encyclopedia of Plant Pathology*. 2 vols. New York: John Wiley and Sons.

Sinclair, W. A., H. H. Lyon, and W. T. Johnson. 1996. *Diseases of Trees and Shrubs*. Ithaca, New York: Comstock Publishing Associates, Cornell University Press.

Stipes, R. J., and R. J. Campana, eds. 1981. *Compendium of Elm Diseases*. St. Paul, Minnesota: APS Press.

Strider, D. L., ed. 1985. *Diseases of Floral Crops*. 2 vols. New York: Praeger Publishers.

Tattar, T. A. 1989. *Diseases of Shade Trees*. San Diego, California: Academic Press.

University of California. 1994. *Pests of Landscape Trees and Shrubs: An Integrated Pest Management Guide*. Publication no. 3359. Oakland: University of California, Division of Agriculture and Natural Resources.

Vittum, P. J., M. G. Villani, and H. Tashiro, eds. 1999. *Turfgrass Insects of the United States and Canada*. Ithaca, New York: Cornell University Press.

Wheeler, H. 1975. *Plant Pathogenesis*. New York: Springer-Verlag.

Yepson, R. B., ed. 1984. *Encyclopedia of Natural Insect and Disease Control*. St., Emmaus, Pennsylvania: Rodale Press.

Appendix B

Glossary

Abscission. Process of shedding or cutting off, as in the shedding of leaves.

Adaptive radiation. Interaction between a host plant and its pest in which a genetic change in the pest allowing it to attack its host plant is matched more effectively by a genetic change in the host plant to counteract that advantage. Also called *coevolution.*

Additive effect. Increase in results greater than what might be attributed to one factor on its own. Used to refer to the impact of disease on plant health.

Aerification. Method of disturbing soil so that air more efficiently penetrates it.

Allelochemical. Chemical produced by a plant that deters feeding by insects or is harmful to them.

Anabolic metabolism. Constructive or building-up portion of metabolism.

Anthracnose. Disease caused by a fungus that forms a fruiting structure and has symptoms of leaf spots, stem cankers, or fruit lesions.

Antibiosis. Category of reduced host plant susceptibility in which a plant produces chemicals that are harmful to the pest.

Antixenosis. Category of reduced host plant susceptibility in which a plant is less attractive to a pest. Also called *nonpreference.*

Apical dominance. Condition where primary growth occurs at the tip of a stem while axillary bud development is inhibited.

Appressorium. Specialized tip of hypha that aids in fungal penetration of the host plant.

Augmentation biological control. Release of purchased natural enemies to control a pest population.

Axillary bud. Lateral bud on a stem that develops at the point where a leaf joins the stem.

Bacterium. A microscopic, one-celled organism that lacks a true nucleus and chlorophyll. Some bacteria cause plant disease.

Biennial. Plant that completes its life cycle in two years.

Biological control. Use of natural enemies such as parasitoids, predators, or pathogens to control a pest.

Blight. Symptom of disease indicating sudden death of foliage, flowers, or stems.

Broad-spectrum activity. Refers to pest control materials that kill a wide diversity of pests.

Catabolic metabolism. Destructive or breaking-down portion of metabolism.

Caterpillar. Larva of a butterfly or moth.

Catfacing. Injury to fruit resulting in uneven growth and deformation, caused by feeding of piercing-sucking insects on developing fruit.

Characteristic abundance. Relatively constant population level that an insect or mite maintains over the long term, due primarily to regulatory processes in the environment.

Chlorosis. Yellowing of plant tissues, often refers to yellowed leaves with green veins.

Coevolution. Interaction between a host plant and its pest in which a genetic change in the pest allowing it to attack its host plant is matched more effectively by a genetic change in the host plant to counteract that advantage. Also called *adaptive radiation*.

Cole crop. Plant in the mustard family (*Brassicaceae*), such as cabbage, cauliflower, brussels sprouts, broccoli, radish, and horseradish.

Compensatory feeding. Increase in feeding associated with a decline in dietary nutrition level.

Conk. Fruiting body of a fungus, resembling a mushroom without a stem, growing on a tree trunk.

Conservation biological control. Any activity—such as reducing the use of pest control materials, providing a nectar or pollen source, or using water sprays to control pests—that preserves, protects, attracts, and retains existing populations of natural enemies.

Control. Containment of a pest population within broad or narrow limits of fluctuation.

Cucurbit crop. Plant in the *Curcurbitaceae* family, which includes gourds and melons.

Cuticle. Waxy layer on the outermost layer of the plant epidermis.

Cutin. Fatty substance usually present in the outer walls of the plant's epidermis.

Defoliation. Loss of leaves.

Density-dependent factor. Factor (such as competition for food and shelter, and the impact of natural enemies) whose strength of effect or disturbance changes in intensity with the population density of the pest.

Density-independent factor. Factors (such as the use of pest control materials, weather extremes, and seasonal changes) whose strength of effect or disturbance on a pest population is independent of that population.

Development. Sum of all the changes that a plant undergoes in life.

Differentiation. Differences other than size that come about during the process of cell, tissue, and organ changes.

Disease complex. Condition in which more than one abiotic or biotic cause of disease is present on a host at the same time.

Disease cycle. Progression of steps involved in disease development.

Disease triangle. Symbol used to depict the three major factors necessary for an infectious disease: a virulent pathogen, a susceptible host, and favorable environmental conditions.

Ectoparasitic nematode. Microscopic, wormlike animal that feeds on plants from outside the tissues, usually an exterior root-feeding nematode.

Endoparasitic nematode. Microscopic, wormlike animal that feeds inside the plant. The entire nematode body may or may not be within the plant tissues.

Endophyte. Symbiotic fungus living in a plant that produces one or more substances that are toxic to animals feeding on that plant.

Epidermis. Outer layer of cells of primary plant tissues.

Epinasty. Downward curvature of plant organs.

Facultative parasite. Parasite that survives primarily on dead organic matter but can survive on live plants for a short time.

Fastidious bacterium. Bacterium that has exacting requirements, usually one which can survive only in the xylem or the phloem of plants.

Floral architecture. Arrangement of petals, stamens, and other flower parts.

Fruiting body. Fungal structure containing spores.

Fungus. Small, thread-like organism that produces spores, lacks chlorophyll, and must subsist on plants, animals, or organic matter.

Gall. Swelling or outgrowth on a plant that is caused by certain insects and diseases. May occur on a stem, flower, or root.

Gallmaker. Organism that creates galls on plants. May be an insect or a disease.

Genetic engineering. Technological process that purposefully changes an organism's genes and/or the expression of the organism's genes.

Genetically modified organism (GMO). Organism whose genes have been changed through a technological process.

Gregarious. Group of many individuals of the same species that conduct functions together, such as feeding, migrating, or molting.

Growth. Irreversible increase in either mass or size of cells, occurring in living organisms.

Guard cells. Two specialized epidermal cells in the plant surrounding each stoma (pore) and regulating the movement of water in and out of the stomata.

Hardiness rating. Rankings of growing zones within the United States based on limits of annual minimum temperatures, with the purpose of indicating which plants can survive winter in each area of the country.

Herbivorous. Obtains energy by feeding on primary producers, usually green plants.

Honeydew. Clear, sticky liquid produced by piercing-sucking insects such as aphids whiteflies, and mealybugs.

Hydathode. Water pore in a leaf.

Hypha. Branch or strand of the vegetative mycelium of a fungus.

Infectious. Able to spread and multiply—generally used to describe a disease-causing agent that can spread from a diseased plant to a healthy plant.

Inoculation. Type of biological control in which small numbers of natural enemies are released over a long time period. Or, the initial contact of a plant pathogen with a plant. Compare *innundation*.

Inoculum. Any part of the disease-causing agent that can initiate infection.

Instar. Form of an insect between successive molts.

Intensive mortality. Selection pressure placed on an insect or mite pest population when pest control materials are used.

Inundation. Type of biological control in which large numbers of natural enemies are released to reduce a pest population quickly. Compare *inoculation*.

Leaf abscission. Formation of a layer of cells at the base of the petiole resulting in the shedding of leaves.

Leafminer. Insect that lives and feeds in leaf cells between the upper and lower leaf surfaces.

Lenticel. Area in the corky layer of stems, roots, and fruit that appears as dots or ridges and is thought to function in gas exchange.

Light duration. Length of time plants are exposed to light.

Light intensity. Amount of radiation that reaches a plant.

Light quality. Spectral composition of light.

Local infection. Small area of infection that usually stays contained near the infection site.

Long-day plant. Plant that blooms when days are long, generally longer than twelve hours.

Mesophyll. Interior portion of a leaf, between the upper and lower epidermis.

Metabolism. Sum of the processes of building up and tearing down the protoplasm as plants develop.

Metamorphosis. Physical changes in form that occur in an insect as it proceeds through its life cycle.

Microsclerotia. Minute, stalked clusters of dark cells that serve as a means of long-term survival of some fungi.

Migratory nematode. Microscopic, wormlike animal that moves through the plant, the soil, or both.

Mite. Small or minute invertebrate, typically with eight legs as adult.

Mollusk. Animal protected by a calcium-rich shell or the remnants of a shell.

Molting. Process of shedding the old skin.

Monocyclic. One cycle—usually a disease with one complete cycle per growing season with no secondary infection cycle.

Mycelium. Vegetative body of a fungus, composed of hyphae.

Mycoplasma. Small, often microscopic cells that contain cytoplasm and nuclear material but have no cell wall. They can cause disease in animals, but not in plants.

Natural control. Maintenance of an insect or mite population over a long time period at a relatively constant level by the combined effects of environmental processes, or density-independent factors, and density-dependent factors.

Nectarthode. Secretory structure found mostly in flowers that excretes a sugary solution.

Nematode. Microscopic, wormlike animal that may be parasitic on plants or animals or may live saprophytically.

Noninfectious. Lacking the ability to spread and multiply—generally used to describe a disease caused by abiotic factors such as moisture extremes.

Nonobligate parasite. Parasite that can grow and reproduce on either living or dead hosts.

Nonpreference. Category of reduced host plant susceptibility in which a plant is less attractive to a pest. Also called *antixenosis*.

Obligate parasite. Parasite that can only survive in or on a living host.

Papilla. Intracellular protuberance of the cell wall. Papillae may slow fungal spread.

Parasite. Any organism that lives in or on another organism, at the expense of the host.

Parasitic seed plant. Plant that can photosynthesize but does not have a root system and must grow on another plant to obtain water and minerals.

Parasitize. Process by which a female parasitoid inserts an egg into a host insect.

Parasitoid. Insect that parasitizes and kills another insect or host. Is parasitic in the immature stage but free-living as an adult.

Parenchyma. Unspecialized plant cells.

Pathogenicity. Ability of a disease-causing agent to interfere with physiological functions of the plant to cause disease.

Pheromone. Substance produced and released by one organism that causes a specific reaction in another of the same species.

Phloem. Food-conducting tissue of a plant consisting of sieve tubes, companion cells, parenchyma, and fiber.

Phloem sieve tube. Series of specialized cells joined end to end to form a tube through which plant food is moved within a plant.

Photoperiodism. Growth response of plants to the duration of light.

Photosynthesis. Plant function in which carbon dioxide, water, and light are used to produce carbohydrates and oxygen.

Phytochrome. Blue-green photoreceptive protein pigment in a plant that senses the day length.

Phytohormone. Plant hormone such as auxin.

Phytoplasma. Pathogen resembling a large bacterium without a cell wall, but causing plant symptoms resembling those caused by viruses.

Plant culture. How plants are grown and maintained in the garden and landscape.

Plant disease. Condition in which a plant differs from a healthy plant as a result of the continual irritation of a pathogen or environmental stress.

Plant pathogen. Living agent capable of causing disease in a plant host.

Polycyclic. Multiple cycles—generally used to describe a disease with more than one cycle per growing season, in which the pathogen continues to increase and spread during the growing season.

Polyetic. Multi-year—generally used to describe a disease cycle that may take several years to complete.

Potential natality. Reproductive rate of a population of individuals in an optimum environment.

Powdery mildew. Fungal disease that produces a white powdery growth on leaves.

Predator. Organism (insect or mite) that attacks and feeds on other organisms, usually smaller and weaker than itself.

Proleg. Fleshy, unsegmented walking appendage on the abdomen of some insect larvae.

Propagule. Unit of inoculum.

Protozoan. One-celled, microscopic animal. Some protozoa can cause plant disease.

Psyllid. Insect with piercing-sucking mouthparts that resembles a miniature cicada. Sometimes called jumping plant lice.

Radula. Feeding apparatus of a slug or snail: a finely toothed tongue-like structure that scrapes through the surface of a leaf.

Regulation. Tendency of an insect or mite pest population to be maintained at a relatively constant level by the action of density-dependent factors.

Resistance. Ability of a plant to avoid damage by a pest.

Respiration. Plant function in which stored carbohydrates are converted to energy.

Rhizomorph. Root-like structure produced by a fungus, such as the strands of hyphae produced with armillaria root rot.

Rust. Fungal disease that gives a plant a rusty orange appearance due to spore formation.

Saprophytic. Used to describe an organism that uses dead plant material as food.

Secondary pest outbreak (pest replacement). Situation in which a major insect or mite pest is suppressed and continues to be suppressed by a particular pest management tactic, but is replaced in importance by an insect or mite pest that was a minor pest initially. Most often occurs as a result of using a broad-spectrum pest control material.

Short-day plant. Plant that flowers during the short days of spring or fall, generally for less than twelve hours.

Signs. Part of a plant pathogen that serves as a clue to the presence of the pathogen, such as visible spores of a fungus.

Skeletonization. Result of feeding by some insects (for example, Japanese beetles) in which the entire leaf is consumed except the veins. Sometimes called window feeding.

Smut. Fungal disease that forms black spores, often in a gall, or galls, on the plant.

Soil inhabitant. Pathogen that can live in the soil without special needs.

Soil solarization. Use of radiation from the sun to eliminate pathogens, insect eggs, and germinating weeds in the soil.

Soil transient. Pathogen that can live in the soil for only short periods and requires a plant host for long-term survival.

Solanaceous crop. Plant in the nightshade family, such as tomato, potato, eggplant, pepper, and petunia.

Stomata. Pores in the epidermis of the plant through which gas exchange occurs.

Stress. External factor that limits a plant's growth and development.

Stress pathogen. Disease-causing agent that infects stressed plants.

Susceptibility. Likelihood that a plant will be damaged by a pest.

Symbiotic. Used to describe a relationship in which two organisms live together for their mutual benefit.

Symptom. Outward expression of disease by a plant.

Systemic infection. Disease infection that moves throughout a plant, usually through the vascular system.

Target pest resurgence. Situation in which an insect or mite population rebounds to greater numbers than before suppression occurred, usually as a result of using a pest control material.

TNSL. Designation that stands for timing, number, stage, and location; an approach to assessing pest problems and determining their impact on plants.

Tolerance. Category of reduced host plant susceptibility in which a plant is able to grow and reproduce when attacked by pests at a level high enough to severely harm or kill related plants.

Translocation. Movement of nutrients or pathogens through the plant.

Transpiration. Movement of water vapor out of the plant.

Trap crop. Plant grown to attract insects or other organisms in order to protect the main crop from attack. Insects on trap crops may act as a reservoir for natural enemies.

Trichome. Outgrowth from the plant surface or epidermis of a leaf, stem, root, or fruit.

Turgor. Tension from internal components giving a cell a swollen or distended appearance.

Tylose. Parenchyma overgrowth into the xylem that provides protection from pathogens.

Umbelliferous plant. Plant that belongs to the carrot family, such as dill, celery, carrot, parsley, fennel, and coriander.

Understory plant. Plant located under the canopy of existing trees or shrubs.

Vector. Agent that moves a pathogen to a plant.

Vernalization. Treatment of seeds or seedlings with a low temperature to influence when plants are mature, often to induce flowering.

VFNT-resistant. Used to describe tomato varieties that are less susceptible to verticillium wilt, fusarium wilt, nematodes, and tobacco mosaic virus.

Viroid. Potential plant pathogen, smaller than a virus, consisting of a single-stranded ribonucleic acid (RNA) without a protein coat.

Virulence. Degree of pathogenicity.

Virus. Submicroscopic entity that is an obligate parasite and consists of RNA or deoxyribonucleic acid (DNA) with a protein coat.

Visible light spectrum. The wavelength of radiation that can be seen by the human eye.

White grub. Thick-bodied larva, or immature stage of various beetle species.

Witches' broom. Broom-like or massed proliferation caused by a dense clustering of branches on woody plants.

Xylem. Water-conducting tissue of plants, often referred to as wood.

Common and Scientific Names of Insects, Mites, Mollusks, and Diseases

Insects, mites, and mollusks

American dog tick	*Dermacentor variabilis*
annual cicada	*Tibicen* spp.
apple maggot	*Rhagoletis pomonella*
ash/lilac borer	*Podosesia syringae*
ash midrib gall midge	*Contarinia canadensis*
Asian longhorned beetle	*Anoplophora glabripennis*
aster leafhopper	*Macrosteles quadrilineatus*
azalea lace bug	*Stephanitis pyrioides*
bagworm	*Thyridopteryx ephemeraeformis*
bean leaf beetle	*Cerotoma trifurcata*
beet leafminer	*Pegomya betae*
billbug	*Sphenophorus* spp.
birch leafminer	*Fenusa pusilla*
birch sawfly	*Arge pectoralis*
black cutworm	*Agrotis ipsilon*
black vine weevil	*Otiorhynchus sulcatus*
blow fly	*Phormia* spp.
boxelder bug	*Boisea trivittata*
bronze birch borer	*Agrilus anxius*

brown speckled leafhopper	*Paraphlepsius irroratus*
cabbage looper	*Trichoplusia ni*
cabbage maggot	*Delia radicum*
carpenter ant	*Camponotus* spp.
carpenterworm	*Prionoxystus robiniae*
cecropia moth	*Hyalophora cecropia*
chinch bug	*Blissus leucopterus leucopterus*
citrus mealybug	*Planococcus citri*
codling moth	*Cydia pomonella*
Colorado potato beetle	*Leptinotarsa decemlineata*
columbine leafminer	*Phytomyza* spp.
corn earworm	*Helicoverpa zea*
corn rootworm	*Diabrotica* spp.
cottonwood borer	*Plectrodera scalator*
cottonwood leaf beetle	*Chrysomela scripta*
cottony cushion scale	*Icerya purchasi*
cypress twig gall midge	*Taxodiomyia cupressiananassa*
diamondback moth	*Plutella xylostella*
dogwood borer	*Synanthedon scitula*
dusky birch sawfly	*Croesus latitarsus*
eastern tent caterpillar	*Malacosoma americanum*
elm leaf beetle	*Pyrrhalta luteola*
eriophyid mite (rose rosette)	*Phyllocoptes fructiphylus*
European alder leafminer	*Fenusa dohrnii*
European pine sawfly	*Neodiprion sertifer*
European pine shoot moth	*Rhyacionia buoliana*
flesh fly	*Sarcophaga* spp.
fall webworm	*Hyphantria cunea*
flatheaded appletree borer	*Chrysobothris femorata*
flower thrips	*Frankliniella tritici*
gray garden slug	*Agriolimax reticulates*
greenbug	*Schizaphis graminum*
gypsy moth	*Lymantria dispar*
holly leafminer	*Phytomyza ilicis*
hollyhock weevil	*Apion longirostre*
honeylocust borer	*Agrilus difficilis*
honeysuckle aphid	*Hyadaphis tataricae*

honeysuckle leafminer	*Swezeyula lonicerae*
house fly	*Musca domestica*
imported cabbageworm	*Pieris rapae*
imported longhorned weevil	*Calomycterus setarius*
introduced pine sawfly	*Diprion similis*
iris borer	*Macronoctua onusta*
itch mite	*Sarcoptes scabiei*
Japanese beetle	*Popillia japonica*
linden borer	*Saperda vestita*
locust borer	*Megacyllene robiniae*
masked chafer	*Cyclocephala* spp.
meadow spittlebug	*Philaenus spumarius*
mimosa webworm	*Homadaula anisocentra*
native elm bark beetle	*Hylurgopinus rufipes*
Nantucket pine tip moth	*Rhyacionia frustrana*
northern fowl mite	*Ornithonyssus sylviarum*
northern pine weevil	*Pissodes nemorensis*
oak leafminer	*Cameraria* spp.
oak spider mite	*Oligonychus bicolor*
oriental fruit moth	*Grapholita molesta*
oystershell scale	*Lepidosaphes ulmi*
painted hickory borer	*Megacyllene caryae*
pales weevil	*Hylobius pales*
peachtree borer	*Synanthedon exitiosa*
periodical cicada	*Magicicada septendecim*
pine bark adelgid	*Pineus strobi*
pine needle scale	*Chionaspis pinifoliae*
pine root collar weevil	*Hylobius radicis*
plum curculio	*Conotrachelus nenuphar*
potato leafhopper	*Empoasca fabae*
redheaded ash borer	*Neoclytus acuminatus*
redheaded pine sawfly	*Neodiprion lecontei*
rose chafer	*Macrodactylus subspinosus*
roseslug	*Endelomyia aethiops*
saddleback caterpillar	*Sibine stimulea*
sawyer beetle	*Monochamus* spp.
smaller European elm bark beetle	*Scolytus multistriatus*

sod webworm	*Crambus* spp.
spruce spider mite	*Oligonychus ununguis*
squash bug	*Anasa tristis*
squash vine borer	*Melittia cucurbitae*
strawberry root weevil	*Otiorhynchus ovatus*
striped cucumber beetle	*Acalymma vittatum*
tarnished plant bug	*Lygus lineolaris*
tobacco hornworm	*Manduca sexta*
tomato hornworm	*Manduca quinquemaculata*
twospotted spider mite	*Tetranychus urticae*
variable oakleaf caterpillar	*Lochmaeus manteo*
walnut caterpillar	*Datana integerrima*
western corn rootworm	*Diabrotica virgifera virgifera*
western flower thrips	*Frankliniella occidentalis*
western spruce budworm	*Choristoneura occidentalis*
white pine sawfly	*Neodiprion pinetum*
whitebanded elm leafhopper	*Scaphoideus luteolus*
whitemarked tussock moth	*Orgyia leucostigma*
yellownecked caterpillar	*Datana ministra*
Zimmerman pine moth	*Dioryctria zimmermani*

Diseases

apple scab	*Venturia inaequalis*
armillaria root rot	*Armillaria mellea*
ash anthracnose	*Discula* spp.
ash decline	disease complex, exact cause unknown
ash ringspot	tobacco ringspot and tobacco mosaic virus
ash yellows	unnamed phytoplasma
aster yellows	unnamed phytoplasma
bacterial blotch of watermelon	*Acidovorax avenae* supsp. *citrulli*
bacterial leaf scorch	*Xylella fastidiosa*
bacterial wilt of cucumber	*Erwinia tracheiphila*
black sooty mold	*Capnodium* spp.

black spot of rose	*Diplocarpon rosae*
botrytis blight of flowers	*Botrytis cinerea*
broomrape	*Orobanche* spp.
brown rot of flowering plum	*Monilinia fructicola*
canker diseases	many genera involved, in particular, *Cytospora* spp., *Botryosphaeria* spp., *Cryptodiaporthe* spp., *Nectria* spp., and *Thyronectria* spp.
cedar apple rust	*Gymnosporangium juniperi-virginianae*
chrysanthemum stunt	chrysanthemum stunt viroid (no scientific name)
citrus canker	*Xanthomonas campestris* pv. *citri*
clubroot of cabbage	*Plasmodiophora brassicae*
crown gall	*Agrobacterium tumefaciens*
cytospora (leucostoma) canker	*Cytospora (Leucostoma) kunzei*
dagger nematode	*Xiphinema* spp.
daylily rust	*Puccinia hemerocallis*
dodder	*Cuscuta* spp.
dogwood anthracnose	*Discula destructiva*
dogwood cryptodiaporthe canker	*Cryptodiaporthe corni*
downy mildew	*Peronospora sparsa*
Dutch elm disease	*Ophiostoma ulmi*
dwarf mistletoe	*Arceuthobium* spp.
elm phloem necrosis/elm yellows	unnamed phytoplasma
fire blight	*Erwinia amylovora*
fly speck	*Schizothyrium pomi*
foliar nematode	*Aphelenchoides fragariae*
fusarium root rot	*Fusarium* spp.
fusarium wilt of tomato	*Fusarium oxysporum* f.sp. *lycopersici*
hollyhock rust	*Puccinia malvacearum*
hosta petiole blight	*Sclerotium rolfsii*
impatiens necrotic spot virus	tospovirus
iron chlorosis	abiotic causes
leafy mistletoe	*Phoradendron* spp.
lesion nematode	*Pratylenchus* spp.
lilac bacterial blight	*Pseudomonas syringae* pv. *syringae*
lilac witches' broom	unnamed phytoplasma

oak anthracnose	*Apiognomonia quercina/Discula quercina*
oak wilt	*Ceratocystis fagacearum*
phytophthora root rot	*Phytophthora* spp.
pine wilt/pinewood nematode	*Bursaphelenchus xylophilus*
pine needle rust	*Coleosporium asterum*
potato spindle tuber	potato spindle tuber viroid (no scientific name)
powdery mildew	many species in the genera *Erysiphe, Microsphaera, Phyllactinia, Podosphaera, Sphaerotheca,* and *Uncinula*
pythium root rot	*Pythium* spp.
rhizoctonia root rot	*Rhizoctonia* spp., usually *R. solani*
ring nematode	*Criconemella* spp.
ring rot of potato	*Clavibacter michiganensis* subsp. *sepedonicus*
root knot nematode	*Meloidogyne* spp.
rose mosaic virus	apple mosaic virus and prunus necrotic ringspot virus
rose rosette	unknown, virus suspect
slime molds	*Physarum* spp., *Fuligo* spp., *Mucilago* spp., and *Didymium* spp., most common
soft rot	*Erwinia carotovora* subsp. *atroseptica* or *E. carotovora* subsp. *carotovora*
sooty blotch	*Peltaster fructicola, Geastrumia polystigmatis,* and *Leptodontium elatius*
southern blight	*Sclerotium rolfsii*
sphaeropsis tip blight	*Sphaeropsis sapinea*
stunt nematode	*Tylenchorhynchus* spp.
tobacco mosaic virus	tobamovirus
tomato bunchy-top	tomato bunchy top viroid
tomato spotted wilt virus	tospovirus
turfgrass patch diseases	*Magnoporthe* spp. and *Gaeumannomyces* spp.
verticillium wilt	*Verticillium albo-atrum* or *V. dahliae*
walnut and pecan bunch	unnamed phytoplasma
white pine blister rust	*Cronartium ribicola*

white rot   *Phellinus tremulae, P. igniarius,* and
                                             Trametes versicolor, most common
                                             pathogens

Appendix D

Metric Conversions

inches	cm	feet	m	feet	m	miles	km
1/10	0.3	1	0.3	200	60	1/4	0.4
1/6	0.4	2	0.6	300	90	1/2	0.8
1/4	0.6	3	0.9	400	120	1	1.6
1/3	0.8	4	1.2	500	150	2	3.2
1/2	1.3	5	1.5	600	180	3	4.8
3/4	1.9	6	1.8	700	210	4	6.4
1	2.5	7	2.1	800	240	5	8.0
2	5.1	8	2.4	900	270	6	9.7
3	7.6	9	2.7	1,000	300	7	11
4	10	10	3	2,000	610	8	13
5	13	20	6	3,000	910	9	14
6	15	30	9	4,000	1,200	10	16
7	18	40	12	5,000	1,500	20	32
8	20	50	15	6,000	1,800	30	48
9	23	60	18	7,000	2,100	40	64
10	25	70	21	8,000	2,400	50	80
		80	24	9,000	2,700	60	97
		90	27	10,000	3,000	70	110
		100	30	15,000	4,600	80	130
						90	140
						100	160

Index

Note: Page numbers in *italic* indicate photographs, illustrations, and graphs.

191